ADVICE TO MEN

'I believe that physical lovemaking should be the visible expression of emotional love. Lovemaking, while a highly skilled and delicate art, only becomes complex if we make it so. Sexual difficulties need not exist, indeed, would not exist, if we did not create them; and the germ and egg of their creation is for the most part ignorance and/or misunderstanding.

'But once we have developed difficulties no amount of philosophy on my part or anyone else's helps. What is needed is practical advice; advice of a kind that can be put into practice.

'That is my aim in this book.'

Also Available

ADVICE TO WOMEN

ADVICE TO MEN

Robert Chartham

A STAR BOOK
published by
the Paperback Division of
W. H. Allen & Co. PLC

A Star Book

Published in 1983
by the Paperback Division of
W. H. Allen & Co. PLC
44 Hill Street, London W1X 8LB
Reprinted 1985

First published in Great Britain by
Universal-Tandem Publishing Co. Ltd, 1971
Reprinted May 1972

Copyright © Robert Chartham 1971

Printed and bound in Great Britain by
Cox & Wyman Ltd, Reading

ISBN 0 352 31247 5

CONTENTS

Introduction

I RECEIVE on average between fifty and sixty letters a week from men and women all over the world, asking my advice on their particular sexual problem. Though the problems deal with all kinds of sexual difficulties there are a number of main categories into which the greater number of inquiries fall; and it is with some of these, as they affect men, that I am proposing to deal in this book.

The more I am involved with people and their sexual problems, the more it is brought home to me that the satisfactory operation of sex is extremely difficult to achieve. If one could go by the statistics provided by my files, for every individual who is happy in his sex-life there are at least five who are unhappy or dissatisfied. I am not putting these figures forward as providing a valid picture of the state of affairs, because more people write to me to tell me they have problems than people who want to reassure me that they have nothing to complain about. Still, the number of individuals with a sex worry must be considerable; and this applies to the Anglo-Saxon cultures, to the Latin and Oriental cultures equally. I am also surprised when I get a letter asking for advice from the sub-continent of India and from the Arabic-speaking world, because these are the countries which respectively produced the *Kama Sutra* and *The Perfumed Garden,* two of the most ancient, as well as detailed, sex-manuals; but letters from these areas do arrive quite frequently, and all indicate that sex-problems vary little in any part of the world you care to mention.

In the main, men's problems centre on their virility. Virility, which is referred to in modern terms as *sexual capacity and performance*, means *male* sexual strength. Its root is the Latin *virilis* meaning *manly, vigorous*. A man's sexual capacity and performance – in other words, his sexual constitution and his ability to perform sexually – means as much to him as the fulfilment of her mother-instinct means to a woman. Though, in theory, the man's ultimate proof to his fellow men that he is a real man depends on evidence of his fertility, i.e. the children he fathers, the woman's assessment of her sexual self is not basically how easily she can be roused or how many orgasms she can achieve in any session of lovemaking, but purely and simply in her ability to conceive and carry in her womb a child to whose rearing she will devote quite a large part of her life.

To be more basic still, a man judges himself, and is judged by others, by the whole of his sexual performance, which, in turn depends on the capability of his sex-members; and this in practical terms means how strong his erection is, how long he can maintain his erection (and specially after he has put his penis into the vagina), how long he can delay coming off and how successful he is in giving his partner a sexual thrill, which he believes, quite without justification, depends on the length and thickness of his penis. Only because his fellows, as a result of our conventions of behaviour, are unable to test these things for themselves by watching him give a practical demonstration of his sexual prowess – that is, watching him actually making love, observing his techniques, timing the various phases of his performance, taking note of the degree of satisfaction he provides for his partner – only because he cannot present his proofs in this way, and because his wife by similar conventions is prevented from giving testimony on his behalf, does he produce the one proof available to him – a child. 'Look,' he proclaims, 'I have fathered a child! This is sure proof, at all events, that I can get an erection; that I am at least a real man. For the rest you will have to take my word, but I do assure you it's all right.'

But he knows that getting an erection is not enough since Marie Stopes and Theodore van de Velde reminded women that they are capable of experiencing orgasm; and not only that, but since they could come off they had as much right to doing so as the man, and should insist on equal experience, that is, an orgasm every time they made love, as the man cannot fail to have. And these same worthies exhorted women to make it clear to men that if they could not produce orgasm in their partners *every* time they made love, they were failures as lovers.

Failures as lovers!

I can think of only one other crime in the field of sexual teaching equal to this one, and that was perpetrated by Sigmund Freud when he put forward the theory of vaginal orgasm, declaring that women who did not experience it after a few years of regular love making were sexually immature.

Masters and Johnson, in their recently published *Human Sexual Inadequacy,* have castigated the thoughtlessness of many high-ranking authorities, who have failed to appreciate what the consequences of some of their pronouncements might be. I find it extraordinary that the 'inventor' of psycho-analysis could have committed such a blunder as this, unless he was deliberately assuring his successors a securer future. Psychology has a far deeper relationship with sex and a far greater influence on sexual performance than most people are aware of. The great majority of cases of sexual dysfunction have no organic causes, but are initiated in and prolonged by the mind exerting its strange influence over our functions and our capability to function.

The effect of the pronouncement that any man who could not sexually satisfy his partner every time they made love was a failure as a lover is at the root of most, if not all, of the male's sexual difficulties today, as it has been for the past fifty years; and I can see no end to it until all sexologists and others who advise upon and deal with sexual difficulties band together to rear a new generation of men who have not been contaminated by this scandalous doctrine.

These last are strong words, I know; but I feel strongly about it; for the fears which generate the majority of men's sexual difficulties are being perpetuated by far too many popular authorities today. It *is* a scandalous doctrine, for the success of it is based on fear, and deliberately sets out to exploit fear. I honestly believe that Marie Stopes's strangely kinked mind devised it to get revenge on men for her failure to achieve a happy sexual life in her first marriage. And how she has succeeded!

There is scarcely a male sexual problem that is not psychologically induced or that does not spring from the man's fear of being rated a failure as a lover. To fail in bed is to strike at the very roots of manhood. It hits a man in his most tender spot – and I don't mean his balls, but in his estimation of himself, and how he wishes to appear to his sexual partner and his fellow men. No man who has not pride in himself can have the self-confidence upon which his general success in life depends.

Before he acquired this fear he had his pride in his sexual prowess. For hundreds of centuries he was not concerned with how he could make love, but how fertile he was as demonstrated by the number of children he produced. Then his male member was not the symbol of his status as a lover, but of his general status in society, gauged by the number of sons he sprang from his loins. Was he happier then? It is strange, but it is significant, that the Old Testament with all its revelations of intimate sexual goings-on, refers to no sufferer of impotence, except perhaps Abraham when he was extremely advanced in years, and that the New Testament is equally barren in this respect. When there were no children the wife's barrenness was to blame, and though this might often have been the result of the husband's sterility, it is never once hinted that the cause was the husband's *impotentia coeundia* – inability to fuck through lack of erection. Who can recall a single major or minor character from the vast panorama of classical Greek and Roman history who was even reputed to be unable to go into a woman? I can't. By the law of averages there must have been some cases of organically caused impotence, but it does make one wonder if psychologically induced impotence is not a fairly modern manifestation.

This accent on male fertility naturally concentrated the man's thoughts on his phallus (erect penis) because only when his penis was erect could he induce his generative seed to leap with uninhibited exuberance from the inner reservoirs of his body. He worshipped his phallus wherever he was to be found – in Israel, Egypt, Persia, Germany and other parts of Europe. 'Show me your man,' Edmund Buckley wrote in his *Phallicism in Japan* in 1895, 'and I will show you his god.' He worshipped his phallus and it served him faithfully; it was not until he transferred the fundamental attributes of the phallus to himself, claiming as his own his phallus's personality, that it began to take umbrage and revenge.

But this is beginning to get too deeply into the subject for my needs here. Let me reiterate: Though man's attention is still focused on his penis and its performance, his reason for demanding its performance to be sound has changed. When he regarded it as the instrument and agent of his fertility, it did not fail him; only when he began to regard it as a means by which he could be judged as a lover did he also begin to experience trouble with it. When he left it to itself it took delight in its function; when he sought to control it through his brain it rebelled. When it took delight in its function it gave him pleasure; now that he too deliberately demands that it shall give him pleasure does it resist.

The man who has been able to avoid the traps laid for him by Sigmund Freud and Marie Stopes and who, while using the arts and skills of making love, does so with a devil-may-care abandon, not caring when one fails but ready to try another if it does, is the man who is free of sexual difficulties. His phallus delights in him because he abandons himself to it; and in its delight it sees he does not fail as a lover. It is the man who concerns himself too much with his reputation as a lover, who ends up by not being able to be a lover at all.

In all my books and articles, while preaching that a man should study techniques to make him a skilful lover, I have insisted again and again that love making should be a happy and gay experience, full of laughter and freedom, uninhibited, knowing no limits. If it is this, I have said, then the serious underlying meaning of it – the symbolic expression of a couple's love for one another – must automatically be realised.

My lovers *cum laude* will tell you that they use their ingenuity to make do with what they've got, and that if they fail once, never mind, they know they will succeed next time. And that is the point – they *know* there is going to be a next time, not that there is going to be a next time if they can make their sexual components operate properly.

I have to admit that now and again I get irritated beyond measure – though I try not to show it – with both men and women who, while madly wanting to be successful in their sex-lives, make such a chore of the whole business. Why on earth, I think, can't they tacitly accept the fact that they are using sex as an experience of love, instead of emphasising it with every stroke of the penis, every flick of the tongue on clitoris, every love-bite, every thrust of buttocks and heave of pelvis? If they would just take this for granted and swing into the delights of spontaneous caress, when they had recovered from the explosion of their climax they could not fail to realise how much they loved one another, for only people in love deeply can make their bodies respond *in excelsis*.

But I realise that a good many people aren't made like that. However, of this I am certain: that it is not only in

their sexual lives that such people have difficulties, and
that sexual difficulties are a pretty certain indication of
problems in other sectors of their lives. It is too commonly
accepted – and I have to admit that I have myself sub-
scribed to the view – that sexual frustrations create other
difficulties. But recently I have become more and more
aware that in quite a large number of cases frustrations in
other compartments of living have been expanded to
embrace the sex-life.

For many, I know, all difficulties begin in bed. When they
do, they spread to out-of-bed activities. Equally many are
in the other category, and in both it is a vicious circle.
This implies especially to the three major sexual concerns
of men – premature or too rapid ejaculation; impotence or
partial impotence; and, though it may not be so evident,
worries about penile size.

All three, as will be readily appreciated, concern the
man because of their connection with and influence upon
his sexual capacity and sexual performance; in other words,
his status as a lover. All three are also easily affected by
psychological reactions of one kind or another. A chance
remark, even a wordless sound of annoyance, uttered
once by the partner is enough to make a man begin to
doubt his adequacy as a lover; and from the very first
moment the seed of doubt is sown, he is in for trouble.
Inadequacy on one single occasion that is not sympathetic-
ally passed off by the partner sets in motion a chain of
events in which *fear* of future inadequacy creates inadequacy
on future occasions.

I am well aware that in my books I have preached a
doctrine of perfection in lovemaking. I have been taken to
task many times for laying such stress on it, being accused
of possibly engendering in my less confident or less competent readers feelings of insecurity which could lead to their
acquiring sexual problems where none existed before.

I am quite unrepentant, however, for most of my
detractors and those who claim that I have done them a

disservice have not read me properly in the first place. (Mind you, neither my detractors nor those who claim I am reponsible for their difficulties are at all numerous; compared with the number of complimentary letters I have received, the critical letters are a tiny fraction, about two in a hundred.) So let me restate here what my doctrine of lovemaking is.

I believe that physical lovemaking, especially between husbands and wives and lovers, should be the visible expression of their emotional love for one another. Since I know no one who is sincerely and deeply in love who is not also completely and utterly in love – in my view, there can be no degrees of loving – it seems to me to follow logically that if one is using lovemaking to demonstrate one's love for one's partner, each and every session should aim at making the physical responses to stimulation as enjoyable and as intense as possible. This applies particularly to the orgasm-sensations, and the way to achieve really intense sensations at coming off is to employ techniques which produce a build-up of pre-orgasmic sensations up to the point-of-no-return. Except on very rare occasions when both partners are on the verge of climax, brought there by a variety of factors, *before* they actually begin to make love, the rapid build-up of sensations and a dash towards orgasm does not produce the really intense orgasm. But, as I have said, these highly passionate encounters do not occur with great frequency.

In brief, it is my contention that the *aim* of every lovemaking should be the production of the most intense orgasm-sensations.

However, everyone is aware that quite often the orgasm-sensations are not highly intense. The reason for this is not faulty techniques, but the intervention of various other factors, such as length of time since last orgasm, health (feeling below par generally), co-operating because one's partner is obviously sexually roused while one is not feeling particularly in the mood oneself, feelings of lassitude or tiredness though not of such intensity as to prohibit one from responding to stimulation to a certain extent, and so on.

In other words, we know that our sexual responses vary in quality and intensity from occasion to occasion.

So I qualify my previous statement thus: The aim of every lovemaking should be the production of the most intense orgasm-sensations that our bodies allow on that occasion.

But this does not provide a let-out for the lazy lover. There should be no falling off in techniques because we feel we can't be bothered. If this attitude is adopted, then lovemaking is not the expression of our love for our partner.

This means there must be a certain concentration in our lovemaking, and this should become second nature after a year or perhaps two of regular lovemaking, so that we concentrate automatically, without it impinging on our consciousness. It is when people 'try too hard' that they are most likely to fail; and this is particularly true when such difficulties exist as partial impotence, premature and rapid ejaculation, and delayed orgasm in the woman.

My doctrine of perfection – and this I wish to stress more than anything else I have said – *is an aim*. Though we strive for it, we know that on many occasions we shall not achieve it. But the whole point is this: *When we don't achieve it, we should not allow our disappointment to engulf us in gloom and detailed self-analysis; but we should say to ourselves 'There's the next time'*.

As one becomes more experienced in practical lovemaking, one of two things can happen. Either we can become careless and slipshod in our techniques, or, our lovemaking will not only be technically good, but also *spontaneous*.

In the early months of lovemaking, I think it is the experience of all but a lucky very few, who are natural lovemakers, that there is very little spontaneity in our sexual encounters. Spontaneity really means 'doing what comes naturally' automatically, without having to think. While one is discovering one's partner's body and teaching her to discover yours, the experimenting which this inevitably entails inhibits spontaneity. It is this lack of spontaneity carried over into sexual maturity which is also an enemy of men and women with sexual difficulties.

One aim in following my doctrine of perfection must, therefore, be to acquire spontaneity. Of course, *experimentation can and should* go on almost throughout the whole of one's sexual life. It is one of the means of defeating that great enemy of prolonged sexual happiness – boredom. But, in later years, a couple won't experiment every time they make love. If they do so a dozen times a year, or even less frequently, it is enough to keep their lovemaking fresh and exciting. It in no way affects the spontaneity of their lovemaking, which is the passport to a problem-free love-life.

If we become careless and slipshod in our techniques we are also setting ourselves on a collision course for trouble; and it is only when trouble has actually met us head on that we realise where we have landed ourselves. Then it is a difficult matter to put right, a slow and often a painful process.

What I am trying to point out is this: Lovemaking, while a highly skilled and delicate art, only becomes complex if we make it so. And we do make it so when we allow our minds to imagine all kinds of things which, while beginning in our minds, become eventually clothed in reality. In other words, sexual difficulties need not exist, indeed, would not exist, if we did not create them; and the germ and egg of their creation is for the most part ignorance and/or misunderstanding.

But once we have developed difficulties no amount of philosophy on my part or anyone else's helps. What is needed is practical advice; advice of a kind that can be put into practice. This is my aim in this book.

However, be this as it may, I shall not be able to avoid

altogether making suggestions that many will find difficult to apply. The success I shall achieve will depend largely on those who come to this book prepared to co-operate.

CHAPTER I

Masturbation

NEARLY FIFTY years ago, when I was not quite thirteen, I was prepared for confirmation by the school chaplain, a young man of twenty-six or twenty-seven. To conclude our course of instruction, we were invited to supper singly by the chaplain, and after the meal he sat us in a comfortable chair, filled and lit his pipe, crossed one foot over the opposite knee – I believe now to conceal his erection – and informed us that he was going to talk to us about sex. He began his chat by giving us a very brief outline of the male and female sexual physiology, including conception, gestation and birth. All this took about ten minutes. For the next half-hour or so, however, his discourse went something like this:

'I've told you that when the man's semen leaves his penis, it is accompanied by the most pleasant feelings. These feelings are one of the things which makes a man want to have intercourse, and is Nature's way of seeing that the human race will go on being reproduced.

'Now, a boy can make his semen spring from his penis and experience these feelings if he rubs the head of his penis with his fingers, or encloses the organ in his hand and rubs it up and down. This is called masturbation, though many prefer to call it self-abuse or self-pollution. Masturbation, like all sex relations between people who are not married, is a grave sin.'

For the rest of the time he debated on this theme. His argument was skilfully constructed and I could see a kind of logic in it. But imagine the effect on a young boy, to whom it had never occurred that the secual activities which he had been enjoying for the past six years, were 'dirty', forbidden by morality, gravely sinful, suddenly to learn that he was deep in moral delinquency!

The trouble was that I and my companions had no experience by which we could have discovered the flaws in his pronouncements. He was an adult, and knew more than we did; and what he said, since he was a priest, must be true.

How could I disbelieve him when he said so solemnly, 'Even if you masturbate only infrequently, you will find that your brain will stop working properly. A boy who masturbates cannot concentrate on his lessons. I believe you intend to be ordained. If you do, you will have difficult examinations to pass before you become a priest, but I tell you here and now, that if you masturbate you will never be able to pass those examinations. Besides, you will be a sinner and a sinner cannot be a priest. Remember that. You will find it will help you when your desire tempts you.'

And finally, there was this horrible last word of warning.

'Because when you masturbate you are wasting God's most precious gift to you – your seed with which he intends you to start new life – He puts certain signs on the faces of masturbators. Grown-ups know what these signs are. I am not going to tell you what they are. But you may be sure that your father, your masters at school, and any grown-up you happen to be with, will know just by looking at you, what you have been doing, and that you are a filthy boy and a sinner who is not fit to live in decent society.

'You will probably think that what I have told you will make life very difficult for you. So it will, but life for grown-ups is never easy. The great thing is, however, that the more difficulties a man has to face, a better man he becomes. We cannot do everything we want to do, nor have everything we want. There are many more ways of sinning than committing one of the sexual sins, and many sins are easier to commit than to resist. But you wouldn't tell lies or steal or kill, would you?

'Well, you must make sure that you don't commit any of the sexual sins, and particularly masturbation. And the picture is not all gloom, because if you keep yourself pure in thought, word and deed now, you will not only know that you are pleasing God, but will find that the sexual relations you have with your wife will be clean and whole and deeply satisfying, because you will be able to give to your wife the deep, pure love that must exist between a man and his wife for them to gain true happiness in marriage. Are there any questions you would like to ask?'

I can recall still the painful effort with which I managed to whisper, 'No, sir'.

I was glad the dark night hid me as I made my way home, and when I arrived I said a curt goodnight to my parents and went straight up to my room, when I fell on my knees and prayed with all the persuasive pleading I could muster, for forgiveness. Tears of anguish poured from my eyes, as over and over again I asked God to forget all the sexual sins I had committed. I reminded Him that I had not known I was sinning and that perhaps this would help Him to forgive me, and I promised Him that I would never sin in this way again.

Presently I quietened. Somehow I became certain that all would be well – so long as I did not sin again, and this I was quite determined not to do. But I had reckoned without the clamant potency of my sex-drive. My struggle with it was not merely a daily occurrence, but a twice, and sometimes a thrice or four-times daily battle. When the urge had me in its grip, if I could possibly do so without being discovered I would kneel down and pray until I felt I had overcome the urge. At night and in the early mornings, however, it was terribly difficult. Even praying did not help then, and sometimes the urge would get the better of me.

When this happened, before the relief of the explosion

had completely died away, I would be overcome with shame and remorse and fear. The mental agony that wracked me then was, I think, more terrible than any I have experienced since. Hours of desperate prayer would follow each fall from grace, and in the morning I would search my face for the visible signs of my sin, and I went to school fully expecting the chaplain to spurn me when he saw the signs.

For several months I wrestled with almost hysterical fervour with this other-angel who had sprung from my loins, and as time passed I did begin to develop a degree of mastery; but it was never complete. Three or four times a week this acute agony of mind and spirit was forced upon me by my unsuitable nature. I would resist until something snapped in my brain, and then I fell upon my penis with a violence that was equalled only by the violence of the orgasm that engulfed me. For a few minutes I turned into the animal I have, in later years, recognised to be me, when after protracted periods of enforced celibacy, I have let lust take control of me.

What would have happened to me I do not know if it had not been for a combination of circumstances, which I need not explain in detail, and which brought me together with a young man in his early twenties. Briefly, I contracted scarlet fever, and for my convalescence my parents sent me to stay with some friends. I shared a room with the eldest boy, John, with whom I quickly established a deep relationship.

I cannot remember exactly how long I had been with these friends before John discovered all about me. It was in the early hours of a Sunday morning. John had been to a dance the evening before, and I had been a long time in bed before he came home.

In the middle of the night I was assailed with such violence that I was awakened by it. It was a particularly strong assault, for, for the first time my waking mind was filled with fantasies similar to those which had accompanied the few wet dreams I had experienced. I tried desperately to put them out of my mind, but they were more powerful than any thought with which I tried to replace them.

It was a long time since I had been so tried, and in the midst of it, the light between the beds was suddenly switched on, and I heard John saying, 'What's the matter, Robert? Are you ill?' and, frightened almost out of my wits, I saw him getting out of bed as he spoke.

'I'm all right,' I told him, 'I think I must have been dreaming.'

'You weren't, you know,' and he smiled down at me. 'You sounded to me as if you're horribly worried about something. You were certainly praying hard.'

'No,' I said. 'It's nothing. I'm sorry I woke you up.'

'You didn't. I haven't been in long. Look, can't you tell me what's the matter?'

He sat on the edge of the bed, and looked into my eyes with such kindness and such understanding in his, as if he had guessed, and suddenly I felt tears rushing to my eyes, and my effort to keep them back was too much for my mind. I turned over on to my stomach so that he should not see them.

He waited until my despair had subsided a little and then he gently turned me back to face him.

'You are in some sort of trouble, aren't you?' he said again; and again the kindness and understanding in his voice was too much for me. Tears flowed, but this time silently, and through them I heard myself saying, 'I don't think I can stand it much longer, and I don't know what to do.'

'Why don't you tell me?' he encouraged me. 'I'm not saying I may be able to help, but two heads are better than one, and a burden shared is a burden halved, and any number of platitudes you care to think of. So, come on, tell me.'

Suddenly I realised I could talk to him. 'I'm in trouble, John, terrible trouble, and I don't know what to do about it, because the more I try the more difficult it seems to get.'

'It's about sex, isn't it?' I nodded. 'I know something about sex. I was your age once, you know, and only a few years back. Why not tell me about it?'

'But it's sinful to talk about sex,' I told him.

He sighed. 'Oh Lord! Has someone been filling you up with that nonsense? I suppose they've told you it's horrible and dirty, too. Well, it isn't, you know. It's something nobody can get away from. It's a very important part of our lives, women's as well as men's. Of course you can talk about it. Sooner or later you have to. But if you don't believe me, well, let's be horrible and dirty for a while; it won't last for long. There's always the bath-tub. Now, come on, just trust me.'

He gave a little chuckle, which, while it did not dispel his seriousness, suddenly seemed to make the perspective less distorted.

'All right,' I said.

I told him everything. He said nothing until I was finished, then he smiled at me.

'You poor old boy! Well, you needn't worry about it any more.'

'But why not?'

'Because there's nothing to worry about. My house-master told us about sex and he said, "There's nothing to be ashamed of, so long as you don't forget you're gentlemen," and I think I'd rather believe him than your priest.'

'But why should priests tell you this, if it's not right?' I asked. 'It's as bad as telling lies.'

'That's another story,' he said. 'Would you like me to tell you the rights of it, if you're not too tired? Or would you rather wait till the morning?'

'I'd rather know now,' I told him.

'The facts first of all, then.'

(Looking back with hindsight, on that night John gave me the first glimpse of his brilliant analytical and logical

23

mind which was to make him, before he was killed in 1941 aged thirty-six, one of the most outstanding professors of urology any British medical faculty has ever known. I often wish he was still alive, because I am sure we should be working together. It was he who more than anyone or anything initiated my interest in sexual behaviour. When I began pioneering sex-education for teenagers half-a-dozen years after this night I am describing, he encouraged me to resist the somewhat bitter opposition projected against me in some quarters.)

So first he told me the facts. He told me about the prodigality of sperms with which we have been endowed, how only one of hundreds of millions unites with the egg, the rest dying, and from this convincingly argued that masturbation, from the point of view of 'wasting God's precious gift', could not be sinful at all. What clinched the argument for me, however, was the sheer logic of the following.

'Husbands and wives don't make love only on those occasions when they want to start a baby,' he said. 'The majority of men and women make love three or four times a week, and if they are not starting a baby, they use something called birth-control, which is one means or another of preventing even one sperm from reaching the egg.'

'You mean french letters?' I asked.

'That's one birth-control method. There are others. But the point is this. Every time a man comes when he's using birth-control *all* the sperms die, just as they do if he comes by masturbating. Our Church does not condemn birth-control – in fact, it seems likely that in a year or two it will actually give it open approval; nor does it say that a man who comes inside a woman in this way is "wasting God's precious gift". But what's the difference? Either way all the sperm die. It's ridiculous to say that one act is sinful and the other not.'

This seemed to me irrefutable, and if I did not accept the views of present-day medical science on masturbation –

which I will set out presently – I would advocate John's views, which were some years in advance of the times, but began to be effective just before the Second World War. I would have done so because they were logical and convincing even if one were not like I was then, clutching at a straw to save myself, as I honestly believed I would, from going out of my mind.

'Don't you agree?' John asked.

'Yes,' I said. 'I'll accept it isn't sinful, but isn't it physically harmful? Won't it affect my mind or cause some other damage to my body?'

I should recall to my readers that it was not until a year or two after the time I am speaking of, that L. G. McGee, in 1927, made the first great breakthrough in the study of testicular secretions, when he extracted an alcohol and other soluble material from a bull's testicles, which when injected into capons restored the male characteristics. Another seven years were to pass before, in 1934, A. Butenandt had found the chemical structural formulae for the two most important male sex hormones (androgens), which were named androstrone and testosterone.

Now, while it had been known that the testicles did secrete some substances besides sperms, it was believed that these substances, whatever they were, became mixed with the semen, and that if the semen was not ejaculated they would pass into the bloodstream and enrich the blood. Conversely, it was believed that if a male masturbated he deprived his blood of these enriching factors, and this would lead to a slowing down of the mental process and weaken the body as a whole. My informant-priest was, therefore, not telling me lies but repeating the popular belief. It was not until the mid-1930s that it was discovered that seminal fluid is what is known as an 'external' secretion, that is, the kind of secretion which, unlike an 'internal' secretion, cannot be absorbed by the body if it is not ejaculated.

This knowledge not being available to John in 1924,

his reply to my question was both coloured by it and yet by his commonsense as well.

'I think you would have to masturbate several times a day to do yourself any harm,' he said.

'What do you call several?' I said.

'Oh, six or seven.'

'What about three or four?' I said.

He looked at me for a moment or two in silence, then smiled, questioned me closely about the frequency of my urges and explained that it was something I would have to accept as unavoidable. 'You'll have to accustom yourself to it,' he said. Then with simple words and examples he explained sexual morality from the Church's point of view – he was a good and sincere churchman, and its application to practical living.

He condemned adultery, but he could not condemn fornication if no one was hurt by it. But he was against promiscuity because 'if you allowed promiscuity then there would be no reason for a man to control himself at all. We have to control our eating and drinking and we have to learn that we can't always have everything we want. We have to learn self-discipline and we can go a long way towards doing this if we learn to control our sexual urges, because if we can control them, it will help us to control our other urges. If we allowed promiscuity, I believe a breakdown of restraint in every activity of our lives would soon occur, and where should we be then?' This he reckoned to be the strongest argument against promiscuity.

'Now about you specially,' he went on. 'Some men's sex-drive is much stronger than others, and it's obvious yours is very strong indeed. You must masturbate and you will have to do it fairly often, because if you don't it will get all bottled up and affect your nerves. I am sure that if you do it twice a day you wouldn't do yourself any harm physically or mentally. But this is what I should try to do if I were you. When your urge is so strong that you feel you just can't resist it, don't try. I reckon that will probably be once a day.

'But when it's not so strong, then fight it. In that way you'll learn to control it, even sometimes when it's very strong; and so you will teach yourself self-control and self-discipline. Whatever happens you must try not to provoke it deliberately in the ways I've told you many young people do, because you have no need to. And do believe me when I tell you that if you give in a hundred thousand times you won't be guilty of any sin. So, for heaven's sake, don't worry. Give it a trial and see how it works out.'

Psychologists will undoubtedly say that I took John's advice because it gave me an easier way out of my difficulties than any other way, and that neither logic nor a conviction that he was right really had anything to do with it. Maybe they are right, I have never thought about it. But right or not, this I do know – as I have grown older and learned more about and become more experienced in the ways of nature, nothing has come my way to make me believe for a moment that John was wrong in what he told me that night.

In my case there could be no doubt that he was right. The mental relief which the easement of my conscience brought me was instant, and indescribable, and it was this release from my imagined burden of guilt that improved me most. It improved me so much, indeed, that though I will not pretend that it was easy to accomplish the restraint John had suggested I should aim for, I no longer joined grim battle with my Angel of Sex. Rather our combats were gaily serious, and after a time I found myself enjoying them, the more so when I began more and more frequently to win.

Throughout my life I have firmly believed that the night John talked to me, and the days I spent with him afterwards, were one of the most important periods of my life. Perhaps I might have shed in some other way the shackles of guilt which the priest had put on me in his brief talk about masturbation, but I doubt it. But this is certain: it was John, and no one else, who freed me once and for all from guilt in any sexual activity in which I have ever been involved and for this I have been grateful always.

I have related this personal experience in the detail I have because it points up two important things in connection with masturbation. First, it shows how an adolescent boy can be overwhelmed by guilt by adults who have a warped idea of the ethics of sexual behaviour and who, in those days, attempted to prevent a boy by fear from using the only outlet he has for sexual tension shrieking for relief. It would not have been so bad had the suggestion been that he should control his masturbatory tendencies because self-discipline is as essential in sex as it is in any other aspect of living – though self-discipline can be overdone. It was the inculcation of guilt and fear that was so terrible, and with its additional implicit, if not explicit, notion that sex is horrid and dirty. Once ingrained in early adolescence, such is the power of the mind, the guilt, the fear and the dirt influenced all sexual activities in adult life, even in happy marriages when the partners' lovemaking had possibilities of being satisfactory. It was only in cases of boys with really penetrating minds that little or no damage was done; as in the case of the young man who wrote to me, 'My housemaster told me that masturbation was sinful and harmful, but I couldn't believe that such a pleasant thing could be either, so I carried on as before, and though I may not go to heaven because of it, at least, after all these years, I have proof that it has done me no harm.'

Second, my story emphasises the change that has come about in the attitude towards masturbation in the past half-century. Now the view is being circulated – and it is a view that has my strongest support – that morals have nothing to do with it, and that far from being harmful, it is mentally and physically beneficial.

The normal outlet for sexual tension is orgasm, and

orgasm is naturally achieved by friction of the walls of the vagina on the penis; in other words, intercourse. But our social structure being what it is, young people between the ages of thirteen and eighteen are denied intercourse. On the other hand, they must have an outlet, and this is easily accomplished by masturbation.

Contrary to general belief, supported by some experts, of whom the late Dr Kinsey was one, the boy's sex-drive, i.e. the number of outlets he requires weekly, is not stronger when he is in adolescence than when he is an adult. A recent survey I have carried out supports my claim on this.* Nor, except in rare cases, does masturbation become a habit. It is true that most boys *periodically* masturbate more frequently than their sex-drive prompts, and do so because it is a new experience about which they are curious – it is this, I think, which has led to the notion that men are most sexually active during adolescence – but over a period they reveal that in adolescence they have no more outlets weekly than they do between the ages of twenty-two and forty, when they are allegedly at the peak of sexual maturity.

In a later chapter I shall be dealing with the nature of the sex-drive. Briefly, our sex-drive is the promptings the sexual chemistry of our body makes by causing nervous tension to build up in our sexual systems. This tension can be relieved only by orgasm with, for men, ejaculation. (Since a woman does not ejaculate, the chemistry controlling her sex-drive is somewhat different, though basically the chemistry of both sexes is regulated by the activities of the sex-hormones.)

This chemical process works at different speeds in different individuals, and it is these different speeds which determine how often we are prompted to make love in response to the sexual tension which our bodies build up. The majority of men experience this kind of arousal about

* *Sex Manners For The Young Generation*, New English Library, price 25p.

three times a week, but there are quite wide variations of frequency experienced by significant numbers of others. Some men, for example, are aroused by their sex-drive as infrequently as once or twice a month, others only once a week: while on the other side there are men who are roused four or five times a week, others who are roused daily, and even some who are roused two or three times a day.

If a man who is unable to have an outlet for his sexual tension through lovemaking and coupling, responds to his sex-drive by masturbating, the frequency with which he masturbates will match the speed at which his particular chemical process works. This will vary, as I have said, from man to man, and it is quite impossible to lay down any hard and fast rule for what may be termed normal masturbating activity.

In these last few paragraphs I have been leading up to the question which exercises the minds of a large number of men who write to ask me, 'Is it possible to have masturbated too much as a teenager?' and who then go on to ask the question that is really uppermost in their minds, 'Do you think my frequent masturbation as a teenager has damaged my sexual system so that I now suffer from ....?' (premature or too rapid ejaculation, or partial impotence, or retarded ejaculation, or a curved penis, or some other difficulty).

When I inquire about their masturbatory frequency in their teenage years I am, in most cases, surprised that it was so low. Usually it is never more than four or five times a week, which seems to indicate that they have responded to a sex-drive of about three times a week – which is average – plus a possible two occasions when they masturbated to relieve a momentary boredom or purely for the pleasure of coming off. This is perfectly natural, for even as adults we make love on quite a number of occasions when we are not responding to our sex-drive. We may be putting the finishing touches to a celebration or an occasion, or suddenly feel particularly loving towards our partners. Adolescents usually masturbate more often than their sex-drive prompts them to do, mainly because the experience of orgasm is a relatively new one, and the pleasant sensations, achieved by no other activity, are so attractive that we are often unable to overcome the urge to treat ourselves to them. And there is no reason why we should resist such urges.

Except in cases of extreme frequency, when masturbation is resorted to as the result of mental illness – and by extreme frequency I mean anything over seven times a day – no harm can be caused to the penis itself or to the sexual system. In fact, the body won't let man ejaculate to excess. As soon as it has had enough, a dragging sensation develops in the small of the back, and the contains of the scrotum begin to ache, and if these have been brought on by masturbation, the penis will become sore. If none of these symptoms occur, then you can be sure there is no excessive masturbation. When they do occur, a couple of days masturbatory inactivity will quickly restore everything to normal.

One thing that can affect the responses of the penis to stimulation is the masturbation technique. This varies from individual almost as much as lovemaking techniques can vary. Some men hold the penis-head between finger and thumb only and draw the foreskin rapidly but lightly back and forth over the glans. Some circumcised men place the thumb lightly under the rim and two fingers on the frenum and rub both rim and frenum gently, some slowly, others very rapidly. Others, however, grip the whole shaft with the complete clasped hand, holding it firmly, and move it up and down so rapidly and violently that one wonders why the penis does not come off in their hands. The men who masturbate in this way whom I have questioned as to why they do it like this, have said they have always done it so and now cannot come off if they try any other way.

Since the men I have talked with have mostly come to me because they were worried by the long time it takes them to come off during normal lovemaking, I have no proof that what I am going to suggest has any basis in fact. But I am beginning to wonder if while using the penis roughly they somehow permanently deprive the nerves in the penis-head of a good deal of their sensitivity, hence the long time it takes them to come off.

There is one technique of masturbating which seems to have this effect on the nerves of the frenum. The penis, instead of being stimulated by the friction of the hand or fingers, is brought to orgasm by no movement of the hand at all. In uncircumcised men the foreskin is pulled right back as far as it will go, and the hand is clasped firmly just below the rim and pushed down towards the pubic-bone and held there until orgasm arrives, which is brought about by the unnatural stretching of the frenum in this way. (Circumcised men use the same technique.) This certainly eventually stretches the frenum so much that even when the penis is erect and not being touched at all, it hangs like a small pouch below the lip of the penis instead of being taut. I have seen three men who used this technique as a regular method of masturbating all with such pouch-like frenums and all complaining that they have difficulty coming off while love-making. As an occasional method, I do not think it can do any harm, but I would advise against its frequent use.

As I have said, apart from these two possible ways in which masturbation might affect a man's sexual performance while lovemaking, neither the physical handling of the penis nor the frequency of masturbation either in adolescence or currently can have an effect on a man's future lovemaking, except psychologically.

The present attitude towards masturbation has now been in circulation for fifteen or twenty years or more, but despite the fact that medical men, psychiatrists and others have been busy publicising it all this time, the number of men, even young men in their early twenties, who have been unable to shed their guilt-feelings about masturbating is quite fantastic. Attitudes may change, but putting into practice what the changed attitudes teach is quite another matter. Men who run into performance difficulties in their adult sexual experience – whether retarded ejaculation or too rapid ejaculation (and there is no evidence at all that any technique of masturbation can cause the latter) – immediately begin to question their former and present masturbating efforts. The more usual form that this questioning takes is that current performance-difficulties are a judgment on them for having masturbated so frequently; which is a variation of the classic guilt-complex (though just as valid) which would formerly have been engendered by the sin attached to masturbation. My 'masturbation' file bulges with letters from young and middle-aged men who all disclose this sense of guilt, though not in so many words; and the unfortunate thing is that once masturbation has been brought into the realms of psychology, it is extremely difficult to disconnect them. This can only be done by the man deliberately compelling himself *to accept* the true facts, which are – let me repeat – that masturbation, far from being physically harmful and morally wrong is physically beneficial and mentally necessary, and no more ethically wrong than making love with contraceptives.

Finally, there is the man who continues to masturbate after marriage, represented by the husband who wrote to me:

Dear Robert Chartham,
    I have been married for four years to a beautiful and wonderful girl who is four years younger than me. (I am 28.) Our sex-life could not be happier or more satisfying. We make love four or five times a week, on average, and every time it seems to be better than it ever was. Please can you tell me, then, why I still

masturbate once and sometimes twice a week as well?
Is there something wrong with me? Am I kinky in
some way? What can I do to stop it?

Unfortunately, he did not say why he is prompted to
masturbate, but I can assure him that he is not alone among
happily married men. Usually a married man masturbates
either because he is temporarily separated from his wife,
or because he is not making love often enough with his
wife, or because the wife is ill, or when there has been a
disagreement or a quarrel which, for the time being, causes
a withholding of any kind of loving word or gesture, and
certainly of sexual activity involving the partner. These
are the most frequent causes of a husband masturbating.

But there are a very large number of husbands who
masturbate for none of these reasons. Sometimes it happens
that the sexual urge suddenly – it seems absolutely without
warning – imposes itself on a man's consciousness. He has
a very firm erection which is almost painful and which is
likely to persist until orgasm is achieved. Why this happens
it is difficult to say, but I have a theory that unconscious
erotic thoughts have speeded up the various fluid-producing
glands and at the same time impinged on that part of the
brain which directs sexual activity. But, however it is
caused, it does happen, and usually at times that are
inconvenient for lovemaking.

Supposing, for example, the husband is having a lie-in,
and the wife is already up, dressed and about her chores
downstairs. Though she would certainly agree to a suggestion that they should make love, the considerate husband
hesitates to put her to the trouble of getting undressed
again, stopping her work and having her schedule inter-
rupted for half an hour or more. Or it may happen while
he is shaving and there is no time to pause for lovemaking.
Or it can happen at the office, where there is no opportunity
in any case. It takes a man only two or three minutes to
relieve the tension by bringing himself off by masturbating,

and the fact that he chooses to do so in this way is neither harmful nor wrong.

I have had letters from wives who have discovered by chance that their husbands do masturbate and are very upset by their discovery because they think they are being sexually inadequate. Certainly, if any husband suspects that his wife has found out he should explain to her that his masturbating is absolutely no reflection whatsoever on their lovemaking. In fact, if a married man does find himself masturbating, I believe that he should not wait for his wife to make the discovery for herself, but should tell her. Explaining to her how men can suddenly be overwhelmed by sexual desire, as I have explained above; or have her read the last three paragraphs. There is nothing to which she should take exception, and nothing which should perturb him. It is a waste of time for him to try not to relieve himself on these occasions.

To sum up: neither adolescent nor adult masturbation, nor masturbating after marriage can be harmful, or is degrading, or is morally wrong. Accepted for what it is — a means of relief from sexual tension — it can only be beneficial physically and mentally. And it has no affect whatsoever on the man's capacity or performance as a lover, except perhaps in the case of the violent masturbator who may suffer from delayed orgasm.

CHAPTER 2

Penis-Size

I DO NOT suppose that many who do not receive the sexual confidences of men are aware of the significance the size of their penis has for a large number. It is not only men with smaller than average penises who can become concerned about penile size almost to the point of obsession. I have before me as I write this, a letter from a man who says, 'My penis when erect is only 8 inches long. I feel I must make it longer. Please can you tell me how?' and I have in my files letters from men whose erect penises measure $3\frac{1}{2}$ to 4 inches who are clearly genuinely concerned, and underlying their concern one can discern not only fear of inadequate performance or of not satisfying their partner, but fear of being laughed at by members of their own sex, and their partners.

This concern about penis-size is almost as old as Man. For hundreds of centuries penile length and bulk have been the yard-stick whereby Man has measured his manhood and had his manhood assessed by his fellows. It was selected for this office because it was wrongly believed that the volume of the ejaculate influenced the size and strength of the children born from it – it was thought that the baby developed entirely from semen and that the mother's contribution was the nourishment of the embryo in the womb, not that she provided the egg – and it was also thought that the bigger the penis the more ejaculate it produced. (Remember that though the discovery of spermatozoa was made by Antony van Leuwenhoek and his friend Hamm in 1677, their function was not discovered until 1856 by the German biologist, Pringsheim.) The erotic art of ancient civilisations has always depicted men with phenomenally large penises, and this convention has been carried down to the 1970s, not only in art of this nature, but in pornographic literature. Men who are concerned with the size of their penises, then, are in a long line of men of all times and races.

In this century concern about penis-size has assumed a new characteristic. Men are now more concerned with being successful lovers than with producing strong and healthy and numerous children. (It would be interesting to know how many couples deliberately check their general health for, say, six months before they plan to start a baby, and determine that they are at the peak of their physical form for that event.) Pride in their sexual adequacy – a very justifiable pride – is still centred in the penis, and it seems that psychologically men who consider themselves under-endowed are particularly vulnerable.

As I have pointed out in previous books, though every penis conforms to a basic shape, its length and girth vary from individual to individual as much as noses, ears, hands and feet vary. There have, however, been numerous surveys of penile length and girth which have purported to be able to establish an average size; and according to these surveys, which tally remarkably closely, the average-sized penis among white men when fully erect measures a fraction above 6 inches in length and about $4\frac{1}{4}$ inches in circumference. There are quite a number of 7-inch penises, but 8-inches-and-above are rare, while the few 9-inch penises that exist ought to be museum exhibits. There are about as many $4\frac{1}{2}$ to 5-inch penises as there are 7-inch-plus penises, while below-4-inches are as rare as 8-inch-and-above.

(By the way, it is important that these measurements are taken along the upperside of the penis from pubic bone to tip, while circumference is measured about one inch below the rim. I point this out, because I have often been proudly informed by the owners of 7-, 7½- and 8-inch penises of their outstanding dimensions, but when I have inquired how the measurements were taken, they were invariably along the side, from the tendon which holds the root of the penis to the groin. When I have asked them to measure again along the top, the somewhat shamefaced replies have disclosed lengths of 5¾, 6¼ and 7 inches. The measurement is taken along the top side because when the pubic bone of the male meets the vagina-entrance no more of the penis can enter the vagina; but though the whole of the top side is taken up, there is always an inch or so on the underside, and at the sides, which do not go in.)

Until a short time ago, it was thought that there was a definite relationship between limp penile length and erect length. It is always difficult to get a true measurement of the limp penis because circulation and the effect of thoughts, of temperature and posture are bringing about changes constantly. Almost all surveys, however, have claimed to establish lengths and circumferences for the limp member – the exception is the survey carried out a short time ago by the magazine *Forum* – the average being given as 3½ to 4 inches long and 3 to 3½ inches round. Since such measurements produced 6·3 inches in length and 4½ inches in circumference, which represents increases of roughly one-third between the two states, these proportional increases were applied to all penises.

The American researchers Dr William H. Masters and Mrs Virginia E. Johnson, however, have recently made an important discovery. After measuring several hundred penises of all lengths, they have reported that it would seem that *the longer the limp penis the less its length increases proportionately in erection than the smaller penis,* e.g. 3½ inches when relaxed may when erect go to 5½ or 6 inches, while the man with the 5- or 6-inch limp penis may have an erect penis of 6½ to 7 inches. They report one case of a 3½-inch limp penis which in erection increased by 120 per cent to 7½ inches; and another of 4½ inches with an erect length of 7 inches.

The great point of this discovery is that it confirms what sexologists have been insisting for a long time – that the man with the small limp penis, which is what his fellows may see, should not let it become a psychological block; and it emphasises that it is the length of the erect penis which counts.

But how far it counts is another matter, too. Let me state here and now and categorically, that the only men who have just cause for complaint are those whose erect penis is 3 inches or less. Anything above this measurement is fully capable of giving any woman complete satisfaction.

Let us examine the facts. The average length of the vagina when the woman is not roused is 3½ inches. Masters and Johnson's researches have revealed that when she is sexually roused, the vagina automatically lengthens by about an inch, or perhaps a little more. This means that the 4½-inch penis completely fills the vaginal barrel. The extent to which the average 3½-inch vagina can be stretched without the woman being more than ordinarily aware of it is 6 to 6½ inches, which represents almost the limit of possible male penetration, the vaginal tissues then being at full stretch. It is only when the vagina is stretched to 7½ to 8 inches that the woman experiences any sensations of stretching, and she may not do so even then.

The only part of the vaginal barrel which is sensitive is the first third of its length, from the vagina-entrance: what Masters and Johnson call the orgasmic platform. It is, therefore, her experience of the penis in this first third which will make any impression on her. Supposing when she is roused her vagina automatically lengthens to, say, 6 inches, which is far in excess of the average. Her orgasmic platform even then is 2 inches long, and a penis of only 3½ inches will make contact with this vital area, with some to spare.

Now, it is a fact that as climax approaches there is often

a psychological desire on the part of both partners for deeper penetration. In my experience, however, and in the unanimous experience of the twenty couples who collaborate with me in various experiments relating to sexual activity and response, this desire is psychologically fulfilled by the partners straining their pubic areas against one another, which gives the impression to both of deep penetration, whether there is actual stretching beyond the normal limit of the vaginal tissue by a 7-inch penis or not. The man with the average 6-inch penis completely satisfies his partner's penetration desire; the man with the 7-inch penis stretches the vaginal tissue to just that degree that is tolerable for the woman; the 8-inch penis goes beyond the tolerance limit, and sets up sensations which very few, if any, women, can accept.

This, by my own experiments, clearly demonstrates that 7 inches is the maximum length which can give a woman pleasure. Anything beyond 7½ inches, i.e. 8 or 9 inches, gives her pain, and if the few 8-inch men will be absolutely honest, they will confess that they do not at any time use the full length of their penis.

In other words, the average 6-inch penis gives really deep penetration, the 7-inch borders on the excessive, while anything above that is useless and might just as well not be there. On the other hand, even the 3½-inch penis makes contact with more than the vital first third of the vaginal barrel in which the woman is conscious of its presence, and can respond to the psychological urge for deeper penetration by the firm pressure of the two pubic areas against one another.

Penile length, therefore, has NO significance whatsoever either in performance or capacity for satisfying the woman. It has significance only for those men who have become obsessed with it. That this obsession can be a very important factor in a man's approach to his whole sexual expression I fully recognise; and because I appreciate the frustrations to which a strong unfulfilled sexual desire can give rise, I have given considerable time to the problem of trying to enlarge the penis.

Before I go on to examine the possibilities of enlarging the penis, let us look for a moment at the penis's structure. The penis is composed of the head, or glans, the shaft (from the rim to the pubic bone) and the root, which is inside the body and consists of the attachment of the penis

FIGURE I

The male internal sex members

A = penis
B = penis-head
C = frenum
D = testicles
E = spermatic cord
F = bladder
G = seminal vesicle
H = prostate gland
K = Cowper's gland

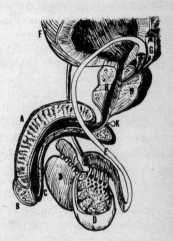

to the front and sides of the pubic arch. (See diagram.) The visible penis represents two-thirds of its complete length.

The whole of the penis, both the visible and out-of-sight, consists of a bundle of three separate cylinders of a special tissue which has erection-making qualities. One of these cylinders, known as the *corpus spongeosum*, forms the under-side – the side which the man cannot see when he looks down at it – and spreads out at the end to form the penis-head. The urethra – the tube by which the bladder is emptied of urine and by which the semen leaves the man's body – runs more or less centrally through the corpus spongeosum. The other two cylinders, called *corpora cavernosa,* lie on top of the corpus spongeosum, their upper ends tucked firmly under the lip formed by the rim of the penis-head with the shaft. (See diagram.) All three cylinders are bound together by skin and tissue, so that it is not possible to separate them except by surgery.

Though the cylinders have different names – *cavernosa* meaning *full of holes,* and *spongeosum, like a sponge,* i.e. also full of holes – and there are slight medical differences, but for our purposes we can treat them as having identical structures.

The penis is covered with skin, ordinary skin, which is like the skin covering the rest of our bodies. The skin of the shaft is what may be termed 'fixed', but that covering the head of the penis, called the foreskin, is loose and can be pulled backwards and forwards over it. The covering of the penis-head is a special kind of membrane, which, in this case, is similar to the membrane lining of the woman's vagina.

Under the skin of the penis is a massive system of arteries and veins which supply blood to it. As soon as a man becomes sexually roused a mechanism is triggered off which pours blood into the penis at a very much faster rate than it can leave it. The blood fills all the thousands of holes in the three cylinders, which has the effect of making the penis swell, stiffen and stand up. So long as the man is sexually roused it will remain in this hard, erect state.

As we have seen, the erect penis is always larger than the limp penis, with regard both to length and girth. This is why the veins and arteries of the limp penis are not straight, but look something like a snake. The loops allow the veins and arteries to stretch when erection takes place. The skin stretches also.

Now, in order to lengthen the penis, the corpora cavernosa and the corpus spongeosum would have to be permanently stretched. Since they are sponge-like in structure, one would think that this ought to be fairly easy to achieve. But the tissue is extremely strong and it is very difficult to stretch it permanently. It is very tough, too, and one would have to subject the penis to very violent treatment indeed before one could do it any great harm. Then in addition to the tissue itself being difficult to distort – because this is what it amounts to – the tubes of the veins and arteries are very tough. Though they can be stretched a little under constant pressure, they quickly spring back to their normal length when released. Even though it might be possible to stretch the tissue, the penis itself would become no larger unless the veins and arteries were also stretched permanently. If stretching does not occur, they are so numerous that they prevent the tissue from expanding.

However, despite all this, about twenty years ago I began a search for some means of enlarging the penis after a young 'patient' of mine became so obsessed by the fact that his penis, $4\frac{1}{2}$ inches long and $4\frac{1}{2}$ inches in circumference, was below average that he eventually had a mental breakdown. With the team of collaborators I then had, and with subsequent teams up to the present time, ever since then I have been trying to find some means of lengthening, or thickening, the penis.

For example, I learned that the Japanese are reputed to use a brick with a hole to take the penis cut through the middle, which, it was claimed, thickened the penis. The brick is heated and the penis is placed through the hole and kept there until the brick has cooled. This treatment is repeated for the space of an hour, two or three times a week.

I had some bricks made to specification, and experimented with six of my team. In my own case it produced a temporary thickening after three weeks' treatment, which disappeared within a week of stopping. A daily application for six months also succeeded in thickening the penis from $4\frac{3}{4}$ inches to $5\frac{5}{8}$ inches, i.e. by just under an inch. Within a fortnight I had lost $\frac{3}{8}$ inch, but did not lose more. The total gain, therefore, was $\frac{1}{2}$ inch, and I do not think that six months' concentration was worth it. Of my six collaborators, only one reported a permanent success after six months – $\frac{3}{8}$ inch.

I then heard of the men of certain African tribes who, from puberty, apply weights to their penises to elongate them. I devised a kind of harness which enabled us to attach weights. We began with a pound for half an hour a day, and after a fortnight worked up to two pounds for half an hour. After three weeks, only one of us had gained $\frac{1}{2}$ inch; the others nothing.

I followed this by making up the recipe in *Kama Sutra*, which recommends boiling pomegranate seeds in oil – it was the only recipe for which we could obtain the ingredients – and massaged the penis with the resultant liquid. All acquired a temporary thickening and some a small increase in length, but none above $\frac{1}{4}$ inch or so, after daily massage for an hour for two months. The extra measurement disappeared in all within a fortnight of stopping.

There were other experiments, none of which were easy to perform and none of which gave any success at all. Finally, however, about two years ago I had a cream made up which contained a hormone ingredient. The penis was first treated with hot towels for ten minutes and then was massaged in a certain way with the cream for half an hour, followed by half an hour's dilation with a vacuum developer.

Out of seven of us, three acquired between $\frac{1}{4}$ and $\frac{1}{2}$ inch in length after three months' treatment, and about the same increase in girth. This increase has remained permanent. The other four had no increase of any kind, temporary or otherwise. Simultaneously with this experiment, a second seven of my collaborators carried out identical treatment, except that they used a theatrical cold cream for massage instead of the special cream. Three reported increases of between $\frac{1}{4}$ and $\frac{1}{2}$ inch, one of $\frac{5}{8}$ inch, which has remained permanent; the other three, no increase at all. It is clear, therefore, that the hormone content of the special cream had no effect whatsoever, and that ordinary cold cream works just as well.

As a result of all these experiments, I have concluded that it is a waste of time to try to enlarge the penis in any respect after a man has reached physical maturity around the ages of twenty-one to twenty-four. At these ages it is just possible to acquire enlargements in a good many cases of between $\frac{3}{4}$ to 1 inch, but I believe, too, that this depends on the penis-structure of the individual. After physical maturity, the increase of $\frac{1}{2}$ inch seems to be the maximum, and that in only a small number of cases. In other words, it is absolutely impossible to *guarantee* a successful result even of these tiny dimensions for *any* individual.

Before puberty, an abnormally small penis can be stimulated into growth by a course of testosterone injections. (These injections do not work in this way after the body has begun to produce testosterone of its own at puberty.) Between fourteen and eighteen development can be acquired by a long course of daily massage carried out in such a way that it stretches the penis constantly throughout massage. After that, up to say twenty-two to twenty-three, attempts can be made, and in certain individuals may succeed; but the older one gets the less likely is success to attend any efforts.

Besides, the longest permanent increase I have recorded is just under $\frac{3}{4}$ inch – in one man. This increase is not long enough to be actually visible to the owner or consciously felt by the partner, and it seems to me that for a man with a $3\frac{1}{2}$ or $4\frac{1}{2}$ inch-long erect penis the addition of $\frac{1}{2}$ inch is not going to be sufficient to help him psychologically, for most men in this category almost invariably set their sights on the average 6-inch penis, thereby hoping for an increase of $2\frac{1}{2}$ and $1\frac{1}{2}$ inches, which, I feel certain, is quite impossible to achieve. I repeat, I maintain I am right when I say that for therapeutical purposes, insofar as medical skills go, it is not possible to increase the size of the penis, except in a very, very few cases. and even then, only when the penis-structure is such to allow it.

In any case, the methods of treatment so far devised require:

(1) Long periods of daily application;
(2) Patient persistence over several months, and this with a very uncertain prospect of success.

I believe it would be helpful if there were expert supervision in the initial stages of the treatment at least, and periodic inspection. But for this a special clinic would be required, and the whole activity could be so costly that it would be priced out of the market except for the wealthy few.

There is also a serious danger that the last state of the patient might be worse than the first. It is not a physical danger, for the penis is a very resilient and strong organ, but a psychological one. In very many minds a course of treatment would create a certainty of success. If it failed, the psychological impact of the disappointment would be tremendous and harmful.

So we come back to 'making the best of what we've got', and I would like to assure my readers that techniques of loveplay and coupling can be devised that can fully compensate for lack of penile length and girth. For whatever anyone says to the contrary, penile girth is not important in the sexual experience of the great majority of women, while those for whom it is important can be taught various techniques to overcome the girth deficiency of their partners, while there are postures and positions which will compensate for lack of length.

However, before I go on to these techniques and positions, I would like to tell those who are embarrassed by the smallness of their limp penis, that I fully appreciate their feelings, because their penis is more likely to be seen by others, except the love-partner, when it is limp.

Let me repeat once again the findings of Masters and Johnson which I stated earlier. *The longer the limp penis is, the less its length increases proportionately in erection.* What this really means is that *it is quite impossible to tell from looking at a limp penis how long and thick it is going to be when erect!* It is the *erect length*, not the limp length, that matters. For all their friends may know, the shy retiring limp penis may take on the proportions of the stallion in the privacy of the love-bed.

When I was at the university, my friends and I were somewhat puzzled by the reputation one of our fellow undergraduates had with women. Nor was it merely reputation; it was only too evident that women wooed him as much as he chased them. The cause of our bewilderment was the size of his limp penis. We were all rowing men, and he was one of the heftiest of us; but one had to look at him hard to see that he had a penis at all. He had a very luxuriant pubic bush, and deep in it the little creature nestled, only its pink head peering somewhat coyly, so it seemed, from the surrounding thicket.

Now and again, when we were in a malicious mood, as young men sometimes are, we used to tease him about it. We would urge him to reveal to us the secret of his success with women. Was it, we asked, that that little thing was not his real weapon, but merely marked the spot where he screwed on his working model, which, we suggested, he kept by his bedside on a bed of dried rose-petals in a cedar-wood box? Or some other ribaldry.

We ought to have given him the greatest psychological block with regard to his sexual adequacy that a man ever had. But he laughed and joked with us, not seeming to care about our taunts at all, and, what could be quite exasperating, with a kind of superior air, as though he had a secret which protected him from our callousness.

Then one summer, one of our group invited two of his cousins to our May Week festivities, and our victim teamed up with one of the girls. Though they did their duty by the party, they spent quite a long time together on their own. Suddenly, however, the girl who had started out jolly and keen to participate in even the most wild suggestions, became quiet, dreamy and preoccupied, and would not go anywhere unless Andrew went too.

'Ah, ah!' commented her host, 'Andrew's been up to his usual tricks! What is the secret of his success? I've a damned good mind to ask her.'

Today we should probably have done just that, but forty years ago, though we might roll a girl in a punt on Granta or Cam, or risk being discovered in bed with her by our college servants, we preserved a kind of reticence about our sexual activities when it came to talking to the opposite sex about them. It was just not done to ask a girl what her partner of the moment possessed that had the effect on her he so obviously had.

However, if we could not ask her, her sister could, if she was willing to. So we took the sister into our confidence, and persuaded Sally, rather like the Philistines persuaded Delilah, to discover Andrew's secret from Jane.

When Sally eventually reported, she said, 'You must be wrong about Andy's tool. Jane says it's bigger than some she's on nodding acquaintance with; but what's more to the point, he knows how to use it for a girl's pleasure.'

(Marie Stopes had recently rediscovered for women that they could come off as well as men, and had an equal right with their partners to orgasmic pleasure.)

We could not believe it. We could not envisage any smaller penis than Andrew's even on a fourteen-year-old boy. Yet we knew Jane was a girl of experience. What did she mean? There was only one way to find out.

We got ourselves somewhat merry – though we were reputed to be quite without shame, this was something we could not do in cold blood – and paid a call on Andrew. We told him what we had come for, and requested him to prove himself. Naturally, he refused; so we overpowered him, stripped him and while the others sat on arms and legs, the fifth stimulated his penis.

After a time, finding he could not successfully struggle against our combined strength, Andrew gave in. 'All right, you bastards,' he said, 'have it your own way! But it'll cost you a bottle of champagne.' We agreed. 'I'll do it myself, too,' he went on. 'Peter's about as much good at it as a boy of twelve.'

I can still recall the scene quite vividly. The five of us rather more sober now, feeling a little guilty – if the others felt like I did – grouped round the naked Andrew sprawled on the settee, the light from a reading lamp on a sofa-table – someone had switched off the ceiling light – falling on his belly, his penis and balls like a spot-light.

'You'd better sport the oak,' Andrew suggested, meaning, lock the outer door so that no one could come bursting in unexpectedly.

Michael sported the oak, and when he came back, he said, 'Don't do it, if you don't want to, Andy.'

'I don't mind,' Andrew grinned. 'I know you chaps have been wanting to know how I manage for ages. Besides, Jane likes champagne in bed.'

Michael got out his pipe and began to fill it clumsily; others lit up cigarettes with nervous fingers. The only sound in the room was the noisy, rather embarrassed breathing of all of us, except Andrew. Presently, as we watched, the little bud-like penis began to emerge from the mass of dark curls in which it was embedded, and within a couple of minutes or so was fully rampant, proud and erect. It did not seem possible, but there was the evidence under our eyes. We had no tape-measure, but it was half as long again as Philip's palm, and he had broad hands – much more than five inches, certainly. But if this was not extraordinary enough, it was swollen to an incredible girth.

'That's the best it will do in these bizarre circumstances,' Andrew said. 'With the proper encouragement he becomes more upstanding and solid. Satisfied?' We told him we were, and had the grace to apologise.

Andrew got up, went to his bedroom and came back in a dressing-gown.

'What about some coffee?' he asked.

We said we would like that. He picked up the kettle from the grate and carried it out to the gas-ring on the landing. While he was making the coffee out of ear-shot, we sat silent for a moment or so, then Robert exclaimed, 'If I hadn't seen it, I wouldn't believe it. It's a freak, of course, a sexual phenomenon!'

We all agreed. Andrew had a unique penis. It was a biological phenomenon, for which there was no rational explanation. We never teased him again. Within a week or two we had got over our wonder at it, and unfortunately I forgot all about it, until I was reminded of it by the Masters and Johnson 'case'.

Those, then, with small penises should not be distressed by what friends and acquaintances may think of it. Even when it is under-average erect, no mere spectator of its limpness can possibly know that it does not double itself when ready for action.

As I said earlier, there are a number of techniques which will compensate for lack of inches both in length and girth, though I would remind my readers that even the $3\frac{1}{2}$-inch erect penis more than penetrates any average-length female orgasmic platform. However, there is often a psychological desire for penetration of some depth in both the man and the woman – the man desires to come as near as possible to piercing, symbolically, his partner's heart; the woman desires to be completely filled.

Let us take girth first. The man can do nothing about this, but his partner can.

A young friend of mine, who had just returned from a trip somewhere East of Suez, once spoke to me in rhapsodies about the lovemaking techniques of the girls he had encountered there.

'There's one thing they do in particular, Robert,' he said, 'which our girls can't do. They can contract and relax the muscles in the vagina so that it grips the penis. One girl I was with could do it so strongly that I couldn't move my penis in and out. The sensation was terrific! Why can't our girls do it?'

'They can,' I told him, 'but it takes a bit of practice. The girls where you've just been are taught lovemaking skills from puberty, even perhaps earlier, and this use of the muscles in the vagina-entrance especially, is one of the skills to which most attention is paid.'

'Couldn't you do something about getting our women to go in for it?' he asked.

I replied that I would do what I could. As a matter of fact, I have briefly referred to this technique in *Sex Manners for Men* and *Sex Manners for Advanced Lovers*, in combination with a similar technique which a man can also learn, which allows him to twitch his erect penis at will by contracting his corresponding set of muscles. But I realise now, that I ought to have been more detailed and more enthusiastic

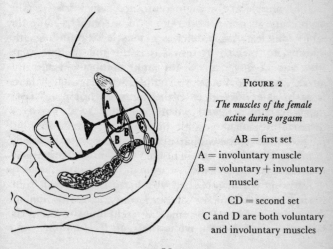

FIGURE 2

*The muscles of the female
active during orgasm*

AB = first set

A = involuntary muscle
B = voluntary + involuntary
muscle

CD = second set

C and D are both voluntary
and involuntary muscles

in my recommendation of it as a lovemaking technique. However, now I have an opportunity to put this short-coming right.

In the woman, the muscles involved are those which surround the vagina, and particularly those surrounding the vagina-entrance. There are two sets of these muscles. The first is a double-horseshoe, which is connected to the interior of the pubic bone. One loop of this muscle encloses the vagina, and the other, and larger, loop encloses the rectum.

The second set forms a figure-of-eight, one loop surrounding the vagina-entrance and the other surrounding the anus. (See diagram.)

The muscles surrounding the rectum and anus – which the man also has – control the emptying action of the bowels. They can be brought into play deliberately by a contraction of the stomach muscles accompanied by a kind of bearing down, or straining. By this contraction, the rectal muscle forces the contents of the rectum down towards the anus, to which the anal muscle responds by relaxing and thus enlarging the opening to allow the faeces to exit.

The muscle at the vagina-entrance, which is especially important in our considerations, is a sphincter, like the anal muscle. (A sphincter is a muscle surrounding and closing an opening or tube.) It is this muscle that keeps the vagina-entrance – as the anal sphincter keeps the anus – closed, so that, for example, when a woman takes a bath, water does not enter the vagina or the rectum. Both openings only expand when persuaded to do so by a penetrating object.

Now, the horseshoe-shaped band of muscle surrounding the vagina and the muscle in the vagina-entrance are only normally contracted when a woman has an orgasm. They go into action then, of their own accord, and nothing the woman can do can stop them. In a great many women, however, these contractions are so slight that she is scarcely aware of them herself, while the man feels nothing, and generally has to ask her if she has come. In other women where the contractions can be felt by the woman, more often than not they can be felt by the man with sensations that seem as though the penis is being gripped. This is especially true of the vagina-entrance muscle.

Although, as I have said, the muscle surrounding the vagina and the vaginal sphincter are normally what is known as involuntary muscles, i.e. they cannot be prevented from acting under certain circumstances, they can by practice be converted into voluntary muscles, that is to say, they can be made to act at the will of the woman *at any time she wishes them to do so.* She is able to make them obey her because they are connected with the rectal and anal muscles, which she can control by bearing down, or straining, as I have described.

If she can learn to control them, then not only does she strengthen them by daily exercises, but by strengthening them she will have three important things happen to her. One, her orgasm-sensations will be much more intense when she comes off; two, she will have provided herself with a lovemaking technique which will make her partner her slave for life (for any man, like my young friend, who has ever had his penis stimulated by the gripping and relaxing of the vaginal muscles, and especially of the vagina sphincter, will testify that it provides an experience of physical ecstasy almost unmatched by any other sexual stimulation; it is impossible to describe the sensations in words; they have to be experienced); and three, *by being able to enclose the penis within the vagina in a tight grip, she can experience that sensation which she sometimes desires and indeed needs, and which cannot be supplied entirely by a penis of under-average girth.* All that is needed to achieve this is the willingness to devote ten minutes or so practice a day to exercising the muscles concerned.

In the past I have suggested the following procedure for doing this. To begin with, the woman provides herself with an object roughly the size of the partner's penis –

preferably a glass tube, obtainable through a chemist — which she inserts in her vagina, having first lubricated it well. By 'bearing down' she compels the rectal and anal muscles to contract, and by doing so automatically forces the vaginal muscles and vagina-sphincter to contract so as to have the effect of gripping the object in the vagina.

At the beginning, and probably for the first week, she will not feel the vaginal muscles and sphincter working at all; but if she perseveres she will in time become conscious of their movement. Each time she carries out the exercise after that, the muscles will make a stronger response.

When she feels the muscles to be gripping quite strongly the object in the vagina, she should replace it by a smaller one — again preferably a glass tube. By trying to make the vagina grip this smaller object she will make the muscles even stronger, and by this method of using increasingly smaller objects, it is possible for most women to be able to grip a single finger or a pencil quite strongly.

My method — the only one I know for strengthening the vaginal muscles — has several drawbacks, however. First, the woman in the initial period, when she may not be able to feel the muscles working at all, may despair and give up. Second, she may find it difficult to obtain an object approximating to the size of her partner's penis — and subsequent smaller objects — if either she or her partner are too shy to ask the chemist for one, though he won't know what it is needed for. Third, she has no means of gauging the strength of the muscle contractions except by how they *seem* to grip the object. This is a psychological flaw in the method, because if she could be sure that her muscles were increasingly becoming stronger, her mind would react so that she made swifter progress, and so lessen the chances of her giving up.

All these drawbacks have been removed by a device that has now come on the market called a Vaginal Muscle Controller (VMC). It consists of a hollow probe made of soft rubber, shaped somewhat like a penis, $4\frac{1}{2}$ inches long and 4 inches in circumference. Since the average vagina is $3\frac{1}{2}$ inches long when the woman is not roused, these measurements have the effect of expanding the vagina, and at the same time provide a thickness which opens the vagina-entrance considerably.

The probe is attached by a tube to a gauge. When the vagina muscles are contracted a needle swings across the graduated face of the gauge and registers the strength of the contractions. Even when the woman cannot feel the contractions the needle registers. Thus, from the very beginning, the woman is given great psychological encouragement. I have carried out tests with a VMC and can personally recommend its use by any woman. Those who can already contract the vaginal muscles will be able to keep them in excellent tone with a VMC. The device is a little pricey at the moment, but if anyone is interested, if they will contact me through the publishers, I will put them in touch with the firm supplying them.

Let me repeat, once the woman has learned to contract the muscles so that she can grip two, or better, one finger, she has not only added a marvellously stimulating technique to her repertoire, but has gone almost all the way to compensating for the imagined physical inadequacy of her partner.

One of the cardinal rules of all men who imagine they have penile inadequacy should be that they never allow themselves to develop a 'pot', A protuberant belly, even on a well-equipped man, has a horrible habit of getting in the way during lovemaking, and it can make quite a difference to depth of penetration.

The other ways in which lack of penile inches can be compensated for, is by the position used in coupling. It is quite surprising how different penetration can be from position to position, and indeed on the same position according to the posture taken by the woman.

For example, in the missionary position, man-above, if the woman keeps her legs flat on the bed, not more than two-thirds of any length penis can go in. But if she draws up her knees, until the soles of her feet are flat on the bed, penetration can be increased by an inch to an inch and a half, while the more she draws her knees up towards her breasts the deeper penetration will be.

If the woman lies over the edge of the bed with the soles of her feet flat on the floor, penetration will be even deeper than in the ordinary man-above position. She must, however, remember to keep her feet firmly on the ground, otherwise depth of penetration will be shortened.

With the woman lying on the man, penetration is shallow. If, however, she kneels or squats astride him, either facing him or with her back to him, and, after the penis has been put into the vagina, sits firmly down on his thighs, penetration will be maximum-plus *provided the woman holds her torso absolutely erect*. If she leans either forward or back even a few degrees out of the absolute straight, penetration is lessened. In this position, the average 6-inch penis can stretch the vagina in such a way that the woman almost faints with the exquisiteness of the sensations. The $4\frac{1}{2}$ and 5-inch penis can also produce stretching sensations while the 4-inch penis seems completely to fill the vagina.

Other positions which also provide maximum depth of penetration, but which do not produce the stretching sensations of the last position, are the rear-entry positions, especially the one in which the woman kneels with her weight supported by her taut arms. The man kneels behind her, between her parted legs. If the woman's buttocks are not abnormally large, the whole of the penis will go in.

A variation of this, is when the woman takes up the same position on a low bed with her feet over the edge of the bed. The man's legs straddle her feet. She opens her legs to allow the penis to be inserted and then closes them and squeezes them together. Penetration is very deep, and by squeezing her legs, she grips the penis and this gives her and her partner a sensation of fulness.

If the man sits on a chair and the woman sits on him with her back to him, very deep penetration is achieved. This will be increased further still if the man opens his thighs and the woman presses her body closer, thereby pushing the penis even further in.

If the woman lies on a table which is on the man's hip-level and he stands between her legs, penetration is deep. It can be increased if she raises her knees until she can cross her feet in the small of his back. The maximum penetration possible, though again not quite with the stretching sensations of the woman-above squatting or kneeling, is achieved if the woman draws her knees up to her breasts, he bends over her and she rests her calves or feet on his shoulders.

Complete penetration is also possible if the man sits on a chair well forward and the woman sits on him side-ways, i.e. she has a shoulder towards him, instead of back or face. While keeping one foot on the floor she raises the leg nearest him.

These are a few of the positions which provide really deep or full penetration, even for the below-average-length penis. There are others which the couple should discover for themselves by experimenting. If, while they are being used the woman brings her vaginal muscle control into play, and the man stimulates the woman's available sensitive zones, their experience and satisfaction will be no less than those of the couple where the male partner has a penis between 4 and $5\frac{1}{2}$ inches.

If those who are concerned with their penile length and girth will try out these techniques they will quickly discover that I am right when I say that a short penis is no less adequate than an average-length, or indeed above-average-length penis.

However, having said all this, I have had a number of cases recently in which the mental distress caused by the smallness of the penis has been so great that I have rightly or wrongly decided that attempts at enlargement can be fully justified if only that they will help to relieve this distress. At the same time, though, I must stress once more that the combination of methods I am going to suggest does *NOT guarantee success for everyone!* Some penises will resist all attempts to stretch them, others may be stretched for a time, but if they are then ignored, they revert to their former measurements.

The method I am going to suggest is the one to which I have already referred and which I and my collaborators found to be the most successful. It is a combination of exercises, massage and the use of a vacuum developer.

A certain firm markets an enlarging course under the trade-name of *Magnaphall*. This consists of:

(1) Exercises which tone up the male sexual apparatus;
(2) Massage of the penis with a specially prepared vanishing cream (which is more satisfactory than the theatrical cream we used).

The same firm also sells a vacuum developer. This is a glass tube fitted with a rubber tube ending in a bulb. The tube is fitted over the limp penis, and when the bulb is depressed a vacuum is created in the tube, which draws the penis while still flaccid up to its maximum erect measurements. After several applications the penis-tissue will begin to stretch by slow degrees – and I do mean slow; no over-night miracle should be expected – and the dimensions of the penis will increase. For the first few weeks the penis will revert to its usual limp size as soon as the tube is removed. It will then begin to stay larger for say an hour, then two, and eventually – we hope – permanently. I have had this tube independently tested by a leading uro-genitary specialist who reported that no damage could be done to the penis by its use, unless the user goes mad and really maltreats his penis.

When we were carrying out our experiments, this was the programme we followed. For the first fortnight, sometime in the evening, we did the exercises, then put hot compresses, as hot as one could bear – *but for heaven's sake, do be careful not to have the water too hot!* – round the penis for about ten minutes. As the compress cooled, so we reheated it. A face flannel, dipped in hot water and wrung out, works very well.

We then applied a liberal application of vanishing cream to the penis, and either standing with legs apart, or on the edge of a hard-seated chair, we began the massage. The action was that of milking, using both hands and beginning each stroke always at the base of the penis, and the hand was pushed away up towards the penis-head. Before the top hand was taken from the penis, the other hand was already grasping the base ready to follow it. Quite strong pressure was applied, and the penis was stretched with every stroke as far as it would go, hurting a little, but not too much. Once the massage has been started the motion of the hands must be continued rhythmically. The rate of stroke should be fairly slow. Some of the group had the co-operation of their wives for the massage, which was even better than self-massage. (Whether we massaged ourselves or were massaged by wives, most of us found that for the first four or five days we all got erections after a few minutes of massage, but we decided, after some discussion, to continue with it, even after we had come, though some whose penises got very tender indeed after orgasm, had to pause for a minute or two until the tenderness had passed. After this initial period, we all found that we did not get erections, however long we continued the massage.)

During the first fortnight, we continued the massage for ten minutes. Immediately after massage, we applied the vacuum developer. As a rule, the penis was so well lubricated by the cream, that we did not have to use a lubricant to get the penis into the tube. Care must be taken to see that the penis goes into the tube quite straight. There is a knack of doing this, which I cannot explain, but it is quite easily acquired in a short time. Some found the best and quickest way to get the penis straight into the tube was to stimulate the penis deliberately until it was erect, then slip it quickly into the tube and wait for the erection to subside, before applying the vacuum. The penis should be stretched by the vacuum until there is a *mild* pulling-aching sensation in the root. The vacuum was applied for ten minutes. At the end of the first fortnight we noticed that the penis was remaining 'inflated' for noticeably longer periods after the tube was removed – between fifteen and twenty minutes. During this first period the whole treatment took about an hour.

For the next fortnight, and always thereafter, we did the exercises in the morning on getting up, and the massage and developer at some time convenient during the day. We increased the massage time and the developer time to twenty minutes. For the remainder of the three months and four months respectively that we kept to our daily programme very strictly, we did the exercises in the morning and massaged the penis for half an hour and applied the developer for half an hour, at some convenient time during the day, but always following massage immediately with developer.

I must stress that the exercises are absolutely vital. In toning up the sexual apparatus, they also increase the blood supply to the penis. This not only gives fantastically strong erections, but keeps the enlarged flaccid penis from reverting to its previous state.

If anyone would like to attempt this method, I shall be glad to supply the name and address of the firm which sells the *Magnaphall* course and vacuum developer. The cost of both together comes to between £7 and £9, because extra supplies of vanishing cream are necessary for three to four months' massage. I will also be happy to advise anyone who may be in need of help. Write to me privately, care of the publishers. Do please take my warning – it may not work for you. But I think that if you wish to enlarge your penis the method stands as good a chance as any, if not better.

CHAPTER 3

'I Come Off Too Soon!'

Dear Robert Chartham, I am 23 and have just got engaged to a wonderful girl. As we are going to be married in about six months, we can't see any wrong in making love now, can you? We make love an average of twice during the week and two or three times over the week-end. It's a marvellous experience for me, or at least it would be absolutely marvellous but for one thing. I come too quickly, so that I am not able to bring my girl-friend off with my penis in her. I am beginning to feel very frustrated, because though I enjoy loveplay – she is marvellous at making love to me – and I always see that she comes off afterwards, there is something missing. In other words, I want to bring her off while we are joined together in the most intimate way a man and woman can be joined. She hasn't said anything, but I am sure she feels the same way. You said in *Sex Manners For Men* that a man must, and can, learn to control his progress towards orgasm, but the more I try, the less likely it seems that I shall ever succeed. Please, what can I do? – L. M.

Dear Dr Chartham, I wonder if you can help me. I am 30 and have been married for three years, and during all that time, except on very rare occasions I have never been able to hold back coming long enough after we've coupled to be able to bring my wife off. Knowing this, I sometimes bring her off orally before

I go into her; otherwise I have to bring her off either with my tongue or finger afterwards. Not being able to fuck properly makes me feel very inadequate sexually. The curious thing is that when I masturbate it takes me anything between two and ten minutes to come off. I must admit that I always masturbated fairly frequently from when I was about 12. In my middle teens, I probably did it once and sometimes twice every day. Do you think this has anything to do with it? I mean, have I damaged the nerves in my penis? But if I have, I can't understand why I take so long to come off by hand, and yet scarcely get my penis in the soft warmth of her vagina when I shed my load. You'd think that if it takes say five minutes vigorous rubbing it would take even longer moving my penis against the much smoother vagina, wouldn't you? I didn't have much experience of lovemaking before I married, probably not more than a dozen fucks. But it always happened then. I've read some- where, I think in one of your books, that though it may take a little time to settle down sexually after getting married, regular lovemaking soon gives one the necessary control. This may be so, but don't you agree that three years, without any sign of improve- ment, is a long time? It isn't just me who's getting fed up; my wife is, too, and if I can't improve soon, I can see serious trouble ahead. So please, please help me if you can! – D. V.

Dear Dr Chartham, I am 56 and have been married 27 years. Until recently our lovemaking has always been satisfactory and very satisfying; not very adventurous, perhaps, but at least it has kept us happy.

About eighteen months ago I suddenly began to come too soon. I wasn't very worried at first, because I believe most men experience occasions when, for one reason or another, they come too soon, as, for instance, if they've been away for a time and haven't made love, or when they've got more than ordinarily steamed up. However, when it kept happening, time after time, I did begin to be perturbed, and lately it has got worse and worse. Before this happened I could hold back five to ten minutes after I'd put it in, but now half a dozen thrusts and it's all over. My wife is sympathetic, though underneath I sense an increasing frustration. Can you tell me why this should happen, and is there anything I can do about it? I hope to God there is, because it is spoiling our sex-lives. – F. T.

These three letters are typical of the pleas I am constantly receiving from young men and men lately entered into middle age. Coming too soon is one of the two or three most common sexual afflictions which plague men. Usually, it is more common among young men, though it does attack men of all ages, and has an unwelcome habit of rearing its unwelcome head at a time of life when other sexual difficulties can crop up.

The medical term for coming too soon is premature ejaculation. But in medical terminology premature ejaculation has a specific definition; it is used by doctors to describe the condition of a man who ejaculates immediately he presents his penis at the vagina entrance, before he has had time to get even the tip of the penis-head through the vaginal rim. None of the men whose letters I have quoted above suffer from true premature ejaculation, which is a more serious condition from the point of view of treatment, and I differentiate between their experience and premature ejaculation, by calling theirs 'too rapid ejaculation'.

Let us get the terms right, then. *Premature ejaculation* is what happens when ejaculation takes place before the penis can be put in the vagina; *too rapid ejaculation* takes place within 30 seconds of the penis being put in the vagina, or, say, a dozen or fifteen swings of the pelvis. In both types, the man's partner is deprived of her orgasm unless he stimulates her clitoris with a finger or orally after he has come. This is not so satisfactory or psychologically rewarding as both coming off, though not simultaneously, during the penis-vagina contact.

The basic factor in the problem, of course, lies in the fact that almost inevitably the man's penis begins to go limp as soon as he has ejaculated, and cannot normally be stimulated to erection again for ten minutes or a quarter of an hour, chiefly because in most men there is a degree of sensitivity in the head of the penis so high that the slightest touch is intolerable. If too rapid or premature ejaculation occurs and the woman can wait until her partner obtains a new erection, and lovemaking can begin all over again from scratch, in quite a large percentage of cases the man will not ejaculate too soon, and the woman will come off while entertaining the penis. There are some couples who are able to overcome their difficulties in this way, but not many. The average woman, who is all worked up and needs only two or three minutes stimulation to take her over the edge, usually fails to respond to stimulation a second time. Her sensations of frustration seem to inhibit her from being able to make a fresh start after a longish pause. (This is not true of the woman who does come off and embarks on a new session of lovemaking as soon as her partner's penis is stiff again.) There are also many men suffering from premature or too rapid ejaculation who are so psychologically upset by their failure that they cannot achieve a second erection; while as many men, after the first orgasm, lose all desire for further stimulation; in fact, they find it so distasteful that any attempt to touch them in any of their sensitive zones, and particularly on the penis, seems physically painful.

However, a number of young men in their twenties, who have come to me for help, have been successful in overcoming their difficulty by masturbating before beginning to make love. Anyone wishing to try this should do it themselves in private, and they should begin lovemaking within five minutes of having masturbated, so that by the time they have stimulated the partner sufficiently for her to be ready to couple, they have lost their penis-sensitivity and can readily be stimulated to erection. Unfortunately, this does not seem to work for those in older age-groups. I think this may be due to the fact that as a man gets older his sexual recuperation process takes longer, and as he may have to wait more than half an hour before a new erection can be induced he loses interest. With the possible exception of the highly sexed, who, even in their late forties and fifties and beyond, are capable of obtaining erection very quickly after frequent orgasms, there are not many middle-aged men whose sexual desire can be sustained for long after coming off. In passing, I have never yet met a highly sexed man who suffered from premature or too rapid ejaculation.

What are the causes of premature ejaculation? Up to now, research into this problem has been very sketchy, but the little we do know seems to indicate that apart from one or two organic reasons, premature ejaculation is in very many cases psychologically induced.

Let me deal with the possible organic causes first. It does seem possible that there are a few men with hypersensitive orgasm-producing nerves in the penis-tip and frenum. When these men are uncircumcised, one would imagine that circumcision, by removing the protective foreskin, would help these vital nerves to become less sensitive. It would appear, however, that the nerves in the circumcised penis do not lose a significant degree of sensitivity. (It is a fact that there are only seconds difference between the average-responsive uncircumcised and circumcised man's progress towards orgasm, the circumcised man being the very slightly slower.) There seems to be little help that one can offer these men, though quite a number who have approached me, and to whom I have recommended the trial of a local anaesthetic, have been much improved.

These anaesthetics come in the form of creams which

contain an anaesthetising ingredient, e.g. lignocaine. A portion, about the size of a rather large pea, is rubbed into the head of the penis and frenum, at least 30 minutes before loveplay starts. An aerosol spray has come on to the market in recent months, however, which is easier to apply and, according to my own tests, more effective than any of the available creams.

The use of cream or the spray does not affect erection in any way. If a cream is used, and the penis is washed well before lovemaking starts, i.e. at the end of 30 minutes, the woman can use oral caress of the penis without experiencing an unpleasant taste. The aerosol spray is tasteless, in any case.

While on the subject of anaesthetic creams and sprays, I must make one or two remarks about their use. Several men to whom I have recommended them have subsequently come back to me to complain bitterly that the creams were worse than useless. Like everything else to do with sex, hard and fast rules about the application of the creams and spray cannot be made to suit everyone. If I say, 'Apply the cream to the penis-head 30 minutes before starting loveplay', it is because with the majority of men it takes 30 minutes for the cream to desensitise the nerves. There may be some men, however, who require the application to be made an hour, or even longer, before the nerves are fully desensitised. Or, there may be some who require double the suggested amount of cream to be applied. It is essential, if the cream does not work as prescribed, that the user should experiment in order to discover his own personal requirements.

There is one physiological cause of premature ejaculation which is difficult to treat. This is when the man has been born with a frenum that is abnormally short. (The frenum, by the way, is the little band of skin on the underside of the penis which joins the ordinary skin of the penis-shaft to the membrane covering the penis-head. The frenum is packed full with a mass of nerves which, if stimulated, bring on erection quickly, and if stimulation is continued, help to produce orgasm.) However rigid the penis is in erection, the skin of the shaft will always move a little, so that even the circumcised penis swinging in the vagina will cause the skin of the shaft to be pushed down as the penis goes forward, and to pull on the frenum. This pulling stimulates the frenum nerves and helps to produce orgasm. If the man with the short frenum is uncircumcised but his foreskin slips backwards and forwards easily, he will be even more susceptible to too rapid ejaculation than the circumcised man, because the action of the foreskin rolling back will exert an even greater pressure on the frenum.

Fortunately, the abnormally short frenum is something of a rarity. I have heard of cases when the condition has been treated surgically so that the frenum does not pull on the penis-head and excite the orgasm-producing nerves. Personally I am rather against this treatment, because the frenum cannot be cut without severing the nerves, and the man is deprived of the service of these nerves. If it should happen that the penis-tip nerves are not very sensitive, the penis deprived of the frenum-nerves will have difficulty in obtaining orgasm. I know of one case when this operation was carried out and the man, instead of coming too soon, was not able to come at all.

I have dealt with four cases of premature ejaculation caused by short frenums, two of which have responded to stretching of the frenum. To do this, the man must induce a really strong erection. He then grasps the penis firmly just below the rim, and pulls the skin of the shaft down towards the pubic bone, stretching the frenum until it begins to hurt a little. He holds the frenum stretched until he feels he may come. He then releases his penis, waits for the imminent orgasm-sensations to subside, and then repeats the process. If this stretching is carried out for five or six minutes daily, after several days the frenum remains permanently stretched, and the man no longer comes off too soon.

Inflammation of the urethral tube and also of the prostate are also organic causes of too rapid ejaculation. The man who suddenly develops too rapid ejaculation after years of normal performance, should visit his doctor with the shortest possible delay. There will be a number of accompanying symptoms, but they are usually so slight that only the trained 'nose' of the doctor will spot them. The most common symptom of urethritis is a burning sensation when urinating and a frequent desire to do so. Prostatitis in younger men can be caused by germs which have moved up the urethra to the prostate. The symptoms are urgency and a frequent desire to urinate, cloudy urine, which may or may not have some blood in it at the beginning and end of urination, diminished sexual desire, incomplete erection or premature ejaculation. The infection can come from sinuses, tonsils and abcessed teeth, and these are usually the cause of prostatitis and the accompanying premature or too rapid ejaculation in men past their forties.

Any man in middle-age who develops too rapid ejaculation should consult his doctor without delay. Prostatitis is easily cleared up by the administration of antibiotics, but the possible cause should be checked so that the return of the complaint can be avoided. With the cure of the prostatitis, the ejaculation trouble will also disappear.

So we come to the psychological causes of too rapid ejaculation, which are present in the large majority of cases. First of all, there is anxiety or fear of various kinds. Let's take anxiety about performance first.

This is generally the cause of too rapid ejaculation in young men, and was what was wrong with the young man in the first letter. He has probably read books that have told him, or he has heard from somewhere, that if he does not bring his partner off with his penis in her vagina, he will be reckoned by her, and anyone else who may get to hear of it, a failure as a lover. This is a tremendous threat to his male concept of masculinity in general and his own

68

virility in general. He gets so anxious about it that he loses what little control he may have. The main factor in his anxiety is his self-acknowledgment that he is inexperienced in sexual techniques. If he can convince himself that when he has had more practice he will be all right, more often than not the anxiety is removed and he learns to hold back. But many men do not seem to have this faith in themselves, and so they are dragged into the bad old vicious circle – the fear of coming too soon makes them come too soon. This is what has happened in all three cases quoted in the letters, but in the first and third there are additional factors.

L.M. chides me, 'You've said in *Sex Manners For Men* that a man must, and can, learn to control his progress towards orgasm, *but the more I try*, the less likely it seems that I shall ever succeed'. This extra factor lies in the phrase, 'the more I try'. The man – or the woman, for that matter – who tries too hard is actually preventing himself from succeeding. In his too great eagerness, he gets himself into such a tizzy that the psychological control he might have is weakened to the point of being non-existent. If only, instead of trying, he would remain calm, forget about his problem, make love to his girl and go into her when she is ready, he could hold back, seconds longer the first time, half a minute longer the next, a minute the next, and so progressing to minutes and eventually full control.

D.V., the middle-aged man, has got himself in the same kind of vicious circle. In his case, the additional factor is a probable prostatitis which he has neglected because the symptoms haven't really bothered him. If he has the prostatitis cleared up, he may still find himself coming too soon, unless he can really be convinced that the complaint was the cause of his too rapid ejaculation. If he can be convinced of it, however, he may be back to normal ejaculation-wise, as soon as the last symptoms disappear; if not, he will be in the same boat as all other too rapid ejaculators.

Other anxieties include fear of catching a venereal

disease. This is the cause in many young unmarried men who shop around for their sex. They could avoid being overcome by this fear if they used french letters, which, while not giving full protection, do give quite a high degree. Once, however, they have got into the habit of coming too soon, they have put themselves on a treadmill, and will have difficulty in getting off, even after they have married and the reason for their fear no longer exists.

Then there is the fear of unwanted pregnancy. Whenever I think of it, I still get a shock: Coitus interruptus (withdrawal) is still, after the french letter and the Pill, the third most popular birth control method (I should say nonmethod) in Great Britain. The number of married couples who are too lazy to do anything about fitting themselves up with a contraceptive is incredible. Consequently, quite a high percentage of withdrawers suffer from coming too soon, which makes their lovemaking all that more risky if they do not want an unwanted child. Fixing themselves up with a reliable contraception could go a long way to helping them overcome their difficulty, but unless they will recognise the fear – and its removal – as the all important factor, they, too, will have joined the vicious circle brigade.

Another cause is just plain fear, sparked off by, of all people, the partner. I think I would not be over-exaggerating if I said that 99·9 per cent of all men have experienced too rapid ejaculation on one or two occasions throughout their lives. It usually happens when there has been a long abstinence from intercourse. The prospect of a good fuck at last is so exciting that all psychological control is lost and the sexual nervous system becomes so stimulated that the slightest attempt at penis-vagina contact brings on immediate ejaculation. If the partner is the wife or regular partner, she will more likely than not be equally excited, and when she finds herself deprived of normal release, she may, in her frustration, say things she will hate herself for afterwards. But afterwards is too late; she has already done the damage. If the man is young and hasn't the experience to ignore her bitter criticism and to laugh off his failure with, 'There's always the next time,' when the next time comes he will be apprehensive about failing again, and ten to one his apprehension will make him fail. The second failure causes him to panic, and sets him going round in the vicious circle.

There are other causes of anxiety, and they all produce the same pattern of too rapid ejaculation. There is one other cause, however, to which I must refer before going on to consider ways and means of trying to treat the complaint.

This cause is resentment against or desire to punish the partner. Usually the resentment or the desire may be subconscious, but it is real enough to cause havoc in the sex-life of the couple.

There are several causes of the resentment, probably the most common of which is the man's assessment of his partner's sexuality and sex-drive being stronger than his own. Or he may find that marriage isn't all he thought it was going to be, resents being tied in a disappointing relationship and putting the blame on his partner, never on himself, he decides either consciously or subconsciously to punish her. Or he may be jealous of one or more of her attributes which may have no connection whatsoever with their sex-life.

He can show his resentment or desire to punish in one of two ways. Either he can come so soon that he prevents his partner from obtaining sexual satisfaction in the normal way; or he can so influence his sexual relations that he never comes off at all, however long he swings or thrusts his penis in the vagina. This last condition, which is the opposite of too rapid ejaculation, is known as retarded ejaculation. It is not so common as too rapid ejaculation, but common enough. The man who uses retarded ejaculation to demonstrate his resentment against or desire to punish his partner is placing all the blame for his not being able to come on her. Unlike the partially impotent man, or the too rapid ejaculator, the retarded ejaculator gets a very stiff erection which he can keep up for three-quarters of an hour or more. Even if he keeps up constant penis movement in the vagina all this time, or allows his partner to masturbate or fellate him, he cannot come off. The tension is there all the time, and creates more frustration than any other form of orgasm impairment. Most retarded ejaculators emphasise their resentment or desire to punish, by maintaining penis-vagina contact or partner masturbation or fellation for half-an-hour or more, then in desperation withdraw and masturbate themselves, when they will invariably come off within a minute. By doing this they are, in effect, saying to their partners, 'You see, it must be your fault!'

The too rapid ejaculator is doing much the same thing, though his approach is different. He is not saying, 'It's your fault'; he is saying, 'You're not worth the trouble. I really can't be bothered to wait for you.' But both he and the retarded ejaculator are subconsciously making their partners the victims of their spite.

Can anything be done to help the too rapid ejaculator? Before I go into possible treatments, let me deal with one or two small but important points. For example, there are some men who claim to be too rapid ejaculators who certainly are not, like the man who told me he always came when he had made about a hundred thrusts, which took him about six minutes. It is important that men should know one of the basic sex-facts of life, namely, the average man who does not try to control his progress towards orgasm and who has not been manually or orally stimulated by his partner, will come off in two to three minutes if he starts to masturbate the very moment his penis has reached full erection, or if he puts his penis in the vagina immediately he has become fully erect. Any man who can maintain penis-vagina contact for two minutes without coming off, is not a too rapid ejaculator, therefore.

Again, many premature or too rapid ejaculators would not be so if, when they couple, the partner parts her vaginal lips and guides the penis into the vagina. If the man is not helped in this way, but tries to gain entrance by pushing his penis in the direction of where he hopes the vagina entrance will be, he will, by doing so, rub his penis-tip against the vaginal lips and pubic bone, which is sexually stimulating. If the nerves in his penis-tip are very sensitive he will come off either before he gets in or immediately afterwards.

Or again, not many men know, it seems, that if, after they have coupled, they tense the pelvic muscles and the muscles in the buttocks while moving the penis backwards and forwards in the vagina, this tensing of the muscles will bring them off much more quickly than they will come if all the muscles are relaxed. There was a time when I could bring myself off just by tensing my buttock muscles and without using any form of direct stimulation of the penis. I used it as a method of masturbating, and I have recently encountered two young men in their late teens who can also bring themselves off in this way.

When the penis is first put into the vagina, the pelvic and buttock muscles should be quite relaxed. The backwards and forwards movement will be a swinging movement, and not the thrusting movement it will be when the muscles are tensed. This swinging movement is just as stimulating for the woman as the thrusting movement is. The man who has taught himself to swing, and has also learned a little psychological control, should be able to keep up the swinging movements for five or ten minutes. Only when his partner tells him she is coming, or after she has come, he can bring himself off literally in seconds of changing from swinging to thrusting and tensing his pelvic and buttock muscles.

Almost without exception, the too rapid ejaculators I know thrust. A number have been 'cured' by learning to swing. Even the too rapid ejaculator can keep up swinging movements for a couple of minutes without coming, and the effect of this psychologically on the man who has always come within fifteen or thirty seconds because he thrusts, is often so great that, encouraged by his success, he can teach himself to prolong the swinging to five minutes or more.

I am of the opinion that even in cases of psychologically induced too rapid ejaculation in which resentment or the desire to punish is the basic cause, ejaculation can be delayed by swinging. But the technique, obviously, works best in those cases where high sensitivity of the penis-tip nerves, or a too short frenum, is the dominant factor.

The man with psychologically induced too rapid ejaculation, is usually best treated by psychotherapy which aims at uncovering and removing the psychological 'block'. This has been the invariable treatment in the past, but recently doctors woking on these cases – notably Masters and Johnson in America, and Dr Alan J. Cooper of the Psychiatric Department of Edinburgh University – have been experimenting with a fair measure of success along predominantly physical lines, with the psychiatric part of the treatment being superficial with the 'Emphasis placed on explanation, education, reassurance, support and developing and maintaining motivation.'*

This form of treatment involves both partners, and without the woman's full co-operation cannot be carried out. She is submitted to the same psychiatric programme as the man, but it is she who plays the major role in the physical treatment of the man. This physical treatment involves the woman inducing full erection in the man, and then masturbating him with her hand until he is almost at the threshold of the point-of-no-return. At this point, he tells her to stop; whereupon she squeezes the penis very hard. To carry out the squeezing she puts her thumb on

*Clinical and Therapeutic Studies in Premature Ejaculation, by Alan J. Cooper, M.D., D.P.M. (Comprehensive Psychiatry, vol. 10, No. 4 (July) 1969.)

the frenum, the forefinger on the diametrically opposite side of the penis-head just *above* the rim and the second finger in line with the forefinger just *below* the rim. She squeezes the penis in this way while she counts a slow five. By five the man's imminent-orgasm sensations will have faded away. She then masturbates him again until he tells her to stop, when she repeats the squeezing. In one training session this is carried out for four or five times.

After a number of sessions of this treatment, the man's ejaculatory sensations should be a little longer in producing themselves than they were before the treatment. The next stage is then begun.

In this, the man lies on his back, and the woman kneels astride him, facing him, with her knees on or slightly below *his* nipple line, and bending forward at about 45 degrees. She then puts the tip of his penis inside her vaginal entrance, and slowly slides her vagina back on the penis. She remains absolutely still until the man feels he may come. She then slips off the penis, takes hold of it and squeezes in the manner presented above until the sensations have died away. The process is then repeated three or four times. This accustoms the man to the feel of what Masters and Johnson call 'intra-vaginal containment', i.e. of the penis in the vagina. Several sessions of this procedure generally lengthen the time that the man can 'hold back' his ejaculating sensations, and when this has been achieved, the woman can introduce movement. She should keep this up until the man is on the point of coming, then stop, withdraw, squeeze and wait. This further increases the man's ejaculatory control, until he should be able to couple and swing for two or three minutes before coming off. With new-found confidence, over a period, he should be able to control his progress to orgasm like any other man.

It is necessary to warn my readers that this is not an infallible cure for everyone. Dr Cooper has announced only a 43 per cent success rate. Masters and Johnson, however, report that out of 186 cases, only 4 failed to learn adequate control. The trouble about the treatment is that it has to be carried out under expert supervision. This means staying in a clinic for a whole fortnight, or attending an out-patients' department for a minimum of twenty fortnightly sessions over a year. Since there are no suitable clinics providing this treatment, and only Dr Cooper is carrying out his researches in one out-patients' department, the chances of Englishmen being cured by this treatment are very remote.

Research along other lines, however, has also proved successful and can be prescribed by any doctor who knows of it. This is treatment by the administration of monoamineoxidase inhibitors, notably isocarboxazid or 'Marplan', as described by Dr D. Bennett, in the *Lancet* (2: 1309), 1961. If the too rapid ejaculator can draw his doctor's attention to the description of this treatment and persuade him to carry it out on himself, he can have hope of a cure.

One last word. I receive more than two dozen letters a week from young men asking me how they can overcome too rapid or premature ejaculation. Quite a large number of these attribute their condition to frequent masturbation during adolescence. It cannot be too strongly stressed that *frequency of masturbation has nothing whatsoever* to do with later too rapid ejaculation. If any too rapid ejaculators would like to try the 'Marplan' cure, they should write to me, c/o the publishers, and I will supply them with details of the treatment which they can take to their own doctors.

CHAPTER 4

Impotence and Partial Impotence

IN THE majority of men, if not all, the greatest sexual fear is that he may lose his ability to have an erection, for apart from the fact that he cannot perform the last phase of intercourse – the putting of the penis in the vagina – or achieve orgasm without erection (or in rare cases only with difficulty), he himself judges his degree of manhood by his ability to satisfy his wife sexually by penis-vagina contact. While the failure to obtain relief from tension by orgasm is bad enough, the failure to satisfy the partner, which is a great slur on his image as a man, is devastating. The loss of erectile power is known as impotence, a term which is applied only to men.

There are two kinds of impotence which afflict men: true impotence and partial impotence. True impotence is when the man cannot get any sign of erection at all. Partial impotence is when the man can get a strong erection during loveplay, but loses it as he tries to couple, or very shortly after getting his penis into the vagina and before he can bring either himself or his partner off.

Let's take true impotence first.

The first point to learn about impotence is that in 95 cases out of 100, it is caused by a psychological block. The other five cases have organic defects, some of which can be treated and corrected, some of which cannot. The psychological blocks are the result of the same kind of outlook or motive such as results in too rapid ejaculation, e.g. fear of one kind or another, feelings of acute sexual inadequacy, feelings of resentment of the partner or a desire to punish her. In the largest number of cases, however, it is fear of becoming impotent that produces the impotence; in other words, the old 'vicious circle'.

While it is true that some young men are unable to get an erection under any circumstances except one, which I will describe presently, it is men on the threshold of middle age who represent the most victims. It is, perhaps, natural that this should be so and for this reason. As a man grows older, not only does his sex-drive lose some of its strength and frequency, but his ability to achieve and sustain a strong erection is weakened slightly. It is when he notices this deterioration that he begins to fear the worst, though in ninety-nine cases out of a hundred his fears are groundless. Despite this, he fears he is going to fail to get an erection and his fear makes him fail; or fails to get an erection on one occasion, panics, fears that he may be impotent next time, and is. The point about this kind of fear-induced impotence is that the cause for the first failure may be very easily corrected. I will come to this presently.

Before going on to consider psychologically induced impotence, let us clear out of the way first the remaining five per cent that have not psychological origins. They fall roughly into two categories: organic impotence and functional impotence, and both can affect the man at whatever age he is.

Organic impotence is due to some anatomical defect in the sexual apparatus. There is a condition of the penis, with which the man is born, known as hypospadias. Hypospadias is a malformation in which the urethra does not continue right to the tip of the penis, but ends in an opening somewhere along the underside. Generally the urethra is too short and prevents erection taking place. Fortunately, most cases of hypospadias can be corrected by surgery, the surgeon making an artificial channel to the tip of the penis. By making this artificial channel longer than the portion of the flaccid penis from the hypospadias opening to the penis-tip, the surgeon makes it possible for the penis to become erect.

If a boy loses his testicles before puberty, or they become diseased, not only will his penis not grow to its mature size, but the childish penis will not erect. (The loss of or damage to the testicles after puberty, does *not* cause impotence for many years.) Another organic cause may be injury to the urethra which has so shortened it that it stops the penis from increasing in length, and so not becoming erect under sexual stimulation.

Disease of, or accidental injury to the brain or the spinal column can cause impotence by preventing the nerves which produce erection from receiving the commands of the brain. Disease of the scrotum, such as hydrocele, i.e. accumulation of fluid in the coverings of the testicles, making the latter appear abnormally large, will stop the penis from-becoming erect.

If any of these conditions or diseases are not too advanced, all will respond to treatment or surgery, and the patient will become potent.

Functional impotence is caused by some disturbance to the proper functioning of the sexual apparatus. Such a disturbance may attack the nerves and interfere either with the brain or spinal cord, or with the tracts through which the nerves run or the endings of the nerves themselves. You see, erection is brought about initially by the centres in the large brain. The messages from the brain to the penis travel down the spinal column to the erection centre, which is a kind of junction-box located about four or five inches above the base of the spinal column. From the erection centre they travel along the sexual nervous system to the erectile tissue of the penis. When these messages are received, the erectile tissue, which is a sponge-like material, fills with blood, which enters the tissue at a faster rate than it leaves it, and the penis becomes stiff and upstanding. Any damage to the nerves along this very extensive route will result in the messages not reaching the erectile tissue, and the penis will remain soft and limp.

All sorts of disturbances can afflict this important nervous system. There may be a circulatory or an inflammatory condition which results in congestion of the sex glands or urethra. On the other hand, there may be a subnormal activity of the testicles.

One of the main causes of functional impotence is exhaustion, which may affect the central nervous system and its associated systems. Exhaustion is less frequently found to be the cause in young men, but is very common among middle-aged and older men. Masters and Johnson list six main categories of causes of the impairment of sexual function in older men: (1) boredom with the sexual partner, (2) preoccupation with career or making money, (3) mental or physical fatigue, (4) over-eating and/or overdrinking of alcohol, (5) physical or mental infirmities either of the man himself or his partner, and (6) fear of failure of sexual performance associated with or resulting from any of the other five categories.

Boredom with the sexual partner is one of the most common causes of male impotence, and one which need never happen. It is not good enough for men to blame their wives for this, by accusing them of lack of interest, refusal to experiment or to couple in any other position but the man-above. Admittedly very large numbers of women are activated by a surfeit of false modesty as soon as sex is mentioned, but it is just these women who rely on their partners always to take the initiative. The young husband should lose no time in converting the excessively modest young wife, by gentle but firm persuasion, to the view that varied sexual activity is not only more exciting, but will stop their marriage from foundering on the rocks of boredom in later years. The trouble is, however, that far too many men, despite all the assistance in the shape of books, are such lazy lovers that it just isn't true; and far too many men, even men of artistic and inventive minds, are singularly unimaginative when it comes to making love. If a couple's sex-life is varied and interesting from the word go, it will remain that way throughout life. To find excuses in the young bride's attitudes to sex is asking for trouble later on.

It is unfortunate that a man tends to be nearing the apex of his career simultaneously with the arrival of middle-age, when the sex-drive and some of the physical-sexual functions are beginning to tail off a little. He is eager to reach the top or, if at the top, to make himself more financially secure against the day of retirement, and in doing so, he so fills his mind with business thoughts that he has little time for other interests, even sex. If only he would shut business out the moment he crosses the threshold of his front-door, and make sex one of his chief alternatives to business, he would be surprised how the mental and physical reaction that inevitably flows from a good fuck, would better equip him for dealing with his business.

Sex, however, is strangely persistent in forcing its attentions on men of all ages. It does so even on the man who has 'dropped out' of sex. He hasn't the energy or desire to be sexually active, but he is nevertheless sub-consciously aware of what he is missing and tries to compensate for his loss of sex by drinking too much or eating too much, or both. He thus successfully launches himself on the treadmill of the vicious circle. He has given up sex because of his other preoccupations and by over-drinking and/or over-eating he makes absolutely certain of undermining his sexual powers more than his preoccupation and the slowing down of his sex-drive could do by themselves. The man who over-drinks and over-eats should correct this failing immediately, and then deliberately restart his sexual activity. He must not expect overnight miracles, however, and he must have the sympathetic and physically active partner to provide him with the stimulation and the stimulus which will persuade his penis to respond.

When physical and mental fatigue are involved, the man who sees them as an excuse not to make love is inherently a sex-lazy man. A physically and mentally fatigued man can always get an erection if he wants to, though it may take a little time for the penis to respond, unless he has a skilled partner who knows how to caress his penis into erectile co-operation, and is willing to. If the partner plays the active part in the lovemaking and the man just lies there and lets her have her will of him – so that he does not add to his mental or physical tiredness – he will experience intense orgasms which will make him so relaxed that the tiredness will quickly vanish, especially if he can sleep afterwards.

If he or his partner has developed some physical or mental infirmity that prohibits lovemaking, the first step must be to remove the infirmity. If the infirmity is a permanent one, then both should take stock and calmly assess the situation and try to work out ways and means of having some sexual activity even if penis-vagina contact cannot be made ever again. If the infirmity, whatever it is, is used as an excuse for discontinuing sex, then the situation is a dangerous one, unless someone can make the infirm partner see that it is the excuse rather than the infirmity which is causing the impotence.

But when all is said and done, it is fear of sexual failure that creates more impotential havoc in those men who are not sexually lazy. In all such cases it is really a misunderstanding of the situation which produces the impotence. In these days of medical sophistication the widespread use of drugs means that practically every ache and pain is dispelled by a drug of one kind or another. Quite large numbers of these wonder drugs affect the sex-drive and cause temporary impotence. This is particularly true of antibiotics and other depressant drugs. Unless the patient realises that it is the drugs that are causing the impotence, the first time the penis refuses to be upstanding he is likely to panic, fearing the worst – that he will never be potent again. Unless he will tell himself that the impotence will only last while he is using the drugs, and that when he has stopped using them all will be well again, he will, by his fear, make himself impotent.

Many cases of long-standing impotence are caused by *one* single failure to achieve erection. Every man experiences impotence at one time or another. The cause may be one of many – a very heavy bout of smoking or drinking, or a temporary dysfunctioning which affects the testicles so that they are unable to produce sufficient quantities of the hormone testosterone, which is responsible for creating sexual desire and influences the erection process (in both men and women). The man who can shrug off one failure, or even two, is in no danger of becoming permanently impotent; on the other hand, the man who is struck by fear of becoming permanently impotent on account of one failure, is almost certainly doomed to permanent impotence.

The usually virile man who suddenly finds himself impotent should first react to the immediate situation, by saying something like this to his partner, 'Sorry, it's not going to work this time. It will be all right next time!' and should finish this up by bringing off his partner manually or orally. Afterwards he should think over what he has been doing lately and try to determine a possible cause from among those I have listed. If he is not able to find one, he should still not worry about his failure. However, after four or five consecutive failures, he should seek medical advice.

There is one type of impotence which can be extremely puzzling. A man may be impotent with his wife, and yet have a strong erection and complete intercourse with another woman. This is a classic case of psychological impotence, and may result from resentment against the wife, fear of what she may say about his sexual inadequacy and so on, though the root may lie in something wrong having developed in the marriage-relationship, which has nothing to do with sex.

The converse of this situation often occurs; that is, a man who is able to make love satisfactory with his wife, but who is tempted to take part in lovemaking with another woman. Quite often, when he has got into bed with the casual partner, he finds himself impotent. This is brought about by feelings of guilt at being unfaithful to his wife, though he may be totally unconscious of having such feelings. The same thing can happen to a single man though the cause of his failure is feelings of sin. Such a man has usually been brought up in a home where sex as a topic of conversation was taboo, or in which one or both parents have given the impression that physical sex is 'not nice'; or he may have developed religious convictions that sex outside marriage is wrong.

Now and again, deficiency of testosterone is the cause of the impotence. The sufferers from this cause are usually late-middle-aged and older men, but some young men can develop the same deficiency. In older men, the deficiency in naturally produced testosterone can be made up by injections or the implantation of pellets of testosterone. This treatment does not work for all men, but all the same this technique has produced quite dramatic recoveries. Unfortunately, this treatment cannot be given to men between twenty and, say, forty-five. The testicles are not the only producers of testosterone; the hormone is also produced, though in much smaller quantities, by the adrenal gland under the direction of the pituitary. If too little testosterone is being produced by the testicles and adrenals, the pituitary urges both sets of glands to speed up production. If too much is being produced, the pituitary orders the testicles and adrenals to slow down production. If, however, testosterone is injected into the patient, the pituitary orders the testicles to stop producing what little they are producing, and after a time they shrivel up, and will never produce testosterone again.

Injections or implantations work in older men because

the testicles have usually stopped producing testosterone altogether. What the testicles cannot produce, the pituitary cannot make them produce, however much it tries. In fact, the shrivelled up testicles of an older man with testosterone deficiency, will begin to enlarge again, and potency will be restored.

Unfortunately, British doctors are not very keen on administering testosterone injections; why, I don't know. Injections are more successful than implanting pellets because quite often a fibrous tissue develops round the pellet, which prevents the hormone from getting into the bloodstream. Injections have the drawback that they have to be given at fairly frequent intervals. But if the man is prepared to visit his doctor every ten days or so, I can see no reason why the doctor should hesitate to see that he gets them.

Can anything be done to correct impotence which is not the result of high testosterone deficiency in older men? In almost all cases yes, provided the cause of the impotence has been discovered. When the possible organic and functional causes have been eliminated, those cases in which a psychological block is the source of the trouble can be treated with psychotherapy. Recently, however, experiments in the Department of Investigative Medicine at Cambridge University have shown that a certain anti-depressant drug can restore potency and sexual desire in quite a large number of cases. In collaboration with a doctor, I am carrying out controlled experiments using this method, and if anyone would like to have details, perhaps they would write to me care of the publishers.

Masters and Johnson have devised a course of treatment which is not dissimilar to that they devised for premature ejaculation. This method relies upon the co-operation of a sympathetic and understanding partner, preferably the wife, but in cases of single or divorced men, a partner well known to the patient. The couple are required to attend, in fact, live in, the clinic for fourteen days, during which time they are encouraged to overcome any inhibitions they might have in their sexual encounters, and the man is taught full muscle relaxation. The partner is taught how to stimulate the man's penis in a 'non-demanding' way. When this has produced an erection which can be sustained for some minutes, 'non-demanding' coupling takes place; that is to say, the penis is put into the vagina but it is perfectly understood by both partners that the man will not be expected to come off. The man lies on his back and the woman faces him, kneeling, bending forward at an angle of 45 degrees, inserts the penis and slides back on it, rather than sits on it. When this has been successfully accomplished at three or four consecutive sessions only then does the *woman* make pelvic movements. This happens on a further one or two sessions, and then the man also makes pelvic movements.

Dr Alan J. Cooper, of the Department of Psychiatry in the University at Edinburgh, has devised a similar treatment in the out-patients department of the hospital. His course covers 20 treatment sessions over a period of a year. Cooper has not had the same high results that Masters and Johnson claim.

The drawback of both treatments is the necessity for the couple to attend a clinic. In fact, the treatment can only be given under skilful guidance, and since there are no clinics for G.P.s to use, it is not very readily available here. I mention it, only to let impotent readers know that research into their problem is being carried out.

What of the man for whom no method of treatment is successful, who is, in other words, condemned to life-long impotence? The main need for restoring erection is to make possible the insertion of the penis in the vagina. For the great majority of couples this is a deep psychological need. It is also a fact that many impotent men can be stimulated to orgasm and ejaculation while the penis is limp. If, therefore, some means can be found of getting the limp penis into the vagina, the couple's problem is practically solved.

Well, there are available two mechanical aids for achieving just this. One is a penile splint consisting of two 'arms' which keep the limp penis straight, and which are kept in place by bands. The other is an artificial hollow penis, into which the penis is placed and which is then inserted in the vagina.

Many medical authorities reject these artificial aids, though I do not understand why. It seems to me perfectly valid that, if medical treatment fails, any mechanical device that will allow the penis to get into the vagina and so fulfil the psychological needs of the couple, should be used. If anyone interested in the two aids I have mentioned would like to write to me care of the publishers, I will let them have details of where they can be obtained.

There is one kind of impotence which is no less puzzling than the full impotence I have described up to now. I call it partial impotence, and every case of it is psychologically induced.

A man begins to make love and has a really strong erection, which he is able to sustain all the way through loveplay. But as he moves to couple, he suddenly loses it; or if he has been able to get the penis into the vagina, it goes soft on him before either partner can come off.

The causes of partial impotance are much the same as those which induce full impotence – resentment against and a desire to punish the partner, feeling of guilt or shame and so on. Many cases, however, have their origins in one particular incident which created fear of discovery just at the crucial moment.

Dear Dr Chartham, (a young man wrote to me recently). When we first got married Jane and I had to live with her parents for a month or two while the repairs to our own house were being completed. We were making love one Sunday morning before getting up and I had only been in Jane for a few seconds, when suddenly a little voice said from the side of the bed,

'Alan, what are you doing to Jane?' It was her nine-year-old brother who had come into our bedroom without knocking, and whom we hadn't heard move across the room because we were both so engrossed in our lovemaking. Jane cried out, I jumped off her. My penis, which had been so stiff that it ached during loveplay, went absolutely soft in a flash.

When we had got rid of the little horror, we tried again. But it was no good, even though we locked the bedroom door. No matter what Janey did to me, I just couldn't get another hard one. We've been in our own house eight months now, and though I know perfectly well we can't be disturbed, because there is no one else in the house, we have never been able to finish intercourse in the proper way. I get a magnificent erection during foreplay, and then when I try to go into Janey, I go all soft – just like that. It's been like that every time we've tried to make love, and we are both going up the wall with frustration. Please, what can I do to get things right again?

This is a difficult case to treat, the more so because the young man recognises the cause of his partial impotence. Psychotherapy is his only hope, and that will probably be a long job, just as it was in the case of another young man who was making love in a field one evening when an old lady walking her dog stumbled on them unexpectedly.

If only both these young men had had the aplomb of the airman and WAAF when I fell over them one misty night on the perimeter of the airfield as I was taking a short cut to my sleeping quarters.

'I'm terribly sorry,' I apologised, 'but I've got lost.'

'That's all right, sir,' the airman replied not interrupting his thrusting, 'I shan't be a couple of minutes, then I'll show you the way.'

I moved a yard or two away, with my back to them. But the girl was as self-possessed as her lover, for very presently

I heard her begin to whimper, and then give a little cry as she came off. Two or three minutes later, a little flushed, but quite brazen – in a nice sort of way – they came over to me, arm in arm.

'Now, sir, you just follow me,' the airman said.

I don't definitely know, because I never asked, but I am quite sure that neither of them had any difficulties of any kind during their subsequent lovemakings.

Almost as common a cause of partial impotence is a deprecating remark made by the partner. She comments, during loveplay, on the diminutive size of her partner's penis, or, if she has not been stimulated enough by foreplay and he does not seem to be helping her at all after he has gone into her, she may quite involuntarily make some critical reflection about his not being much of a lover. To be told he is inadequate makes him totally inadequate, and future fear of criticism or of being inadequate makes him unable to keep his erection long enough to bring either his partner or himself off. The unfortunate thing about it is that he will thereafter, no matter how sorry she may be that she spoke, be afraid of being inadequate with all women, and his fear makes him inadequate.

To conclude on a more encouraging note: All cases of specifically psychologically caused impotence and partial impotence are capable of recovery if the victim is prepared to co-operate two hundred per cent with his therapist, and if he has a partner who truly understands his problem and is prepared to co-operate also. The treatment may be long, often tedious, often disheartening – but determination can overcome all these.

So long as the penis is capable of erection in any way, there is hope. The best test is 'morning erections', the spontaneous erection a man finds he has on waking. If he has morning erections, then he cannot be truly impotent, even though he may not respond to any form of stimulation.

CHAPTER 5

Circumcision

DURING ONE of the spells of schoolmastering I endured, I was 'on duty' one day and all of a sudden became aware of an ominous silence that was being emitted from one of the changing-rooms, where twenty-two small boys between the ages of eleven and thirteen were supposed to be changing after a game of football. Not only suspicious but curious, I went quietly to the room, which I was able to enter un-noticed

Twenty-one of the boys, stark naked, were lined up against their lockers, and the remaining boy was going slowly along the line, examining his friends' penises very closely, fingering each one lightly in order to satisfy himself of the presence or absence of a foreskin. Those with foreskins he dubbed Cavaliers; those who were circumcised he dubbed Roundheads.

I did nothing to break up the scene until he had reached the end of the line, when I quietly asked why he was making his inspection. When the shock of finding me present had subsided, he explained that they were organising a game of Roundheads and Cavaliers for whiling away the after-lunch break. The trouble was that no one could really make up his mind which side he wanted to be on, and he thought that this would be a good way of settling any arguments.

'But supposing,' I asked him, 'a boy who has been circumcised and dubbed a Roundhead by you is really and truly a Cavalier by conviction? Are you going to compel him to be a Roundhead against his conscience? If so, I think you are going to be in for trouble.'

'In what way, sir?'

'You are inviting, in fact you are insisting on, a traitor coming into your camp.'

'Yes, I suppose you are right, sir. I hadn't thought of that. In any case, the idea doesn't work, because there are four more Roundheads than Cavaliers.'

'Please, sir,' another boy piped up, 'why are some boys circumcised and others not?'

'I wish I was circumcised!' said a third.

I always made it a rule to tell my charges whatever they wanted to know. If I was not primed already to give them a full answer, I would tell them so, promise to find out what I could, and give them the answer later.

I was not primed in this case, because it had never occurred to me that circumcision or uncircumcision was the subject of personal tastes. Why did some parents have their sons circumcised, while others did not? Why did some uncircumcised men wish they were circumcised, and some circumcised wish they were not? However, when I began to go into the question in order to keep my promise, I quickly discovered that the subject generates quite a lot of heat on both sides.

Consider the following letters which appeared at intervals in the magazine *Forum*:

Recently *The Times* contained an article observing the difficulties faced by both parents in having their sons circumcised and emphasising how unnecessary it is in almost every case.

Surely it is about time that this cruel mutilation of the male genitals was made illegal unless and until the young male is both physically and mentally able to decide for himself (as in the case of tattooing); except possibly when a principle or family religion is involved.

As a mutilated male I can only add that the pleasures of being fellated (as so often advocated by Mr Chartham) are completely unknown to me, owing to the almost total insensitivity of my glans due to constant exposure and dryness, despite the fact that my frenum is intact. Furthermore, the intense and prolonged activity required to reach orgasm is both frustrating and induces a feeling of despairing inadequacy throughout.

Mr Chartham advocated the complete retraction of the foreskin before fellation is begun if it is to be completely enjoyed. However, none of my uncircumcised colleagues have confirmed this to be the case since the glans itself is too sensitive for preliminary direct stimulation, and this quickly results in premature ejaculation.

I feel sure that most would agree that the most sensuous sensations are achieved when the foreskin is drawn forward and back over the moist erect penis, only partly exposing the glans in the process. Complete exposure of the glans should only occur after intromission and as the climax of the vigorous and involuntary thrusts to this end.

From this I conclude that the longer the foreskin the greater the sensations and pleasures of true virility. – F.H.

To this F.C. replied:

F.H. wonders how many men would agree with him that circumcision is a mutilation. I can assure him from my own experience that literally hundreds of thousands would. All the handicaps he mentions, caused solely by this damnable interference with our sexual efficiency, are very commonly maddening to a vast army of silent suffering victims of this criminal atrocity which is still being perpetrated in this so-called 'enlightened' age.

The decision regarding the destruction of this very important and very useful appendage, most often left to the whim of the mother, should very definitely not be the prerogative of the parents. At least 90 per cent of the unfortunate males who have been so cruelly deprived of this miraculous structure would not have elected to part with it if it had been left to them to decide for themselves.

I for one would readily join the throng of men who would queue for the re-grafting of a new foreskin by surgery, if it ever became a real possibility. The advantages of this scientific fold of skin (provided so benevolently by nature) are numerous and manifold. It is of vital importance for the full enjoyment of tactile feelings during coitus. Therefore, anyone with a long foreskin which is perhaps a full inch beyond the tip of the glans is indeed lucky, by virtue of the fact that he should be able to achieve full erection with the glans still remaining completely covered by the skin. The inner layer is thereby a somewhat larger 'area' of delicate sensitivity to come in contact with the moist vaginal surface as it rolls off the knob during the initial thrust of the penis . . . .

I feel sure a large number of the lads who are so clamorous in their endeavour to become circumcised would surely 'think again' about it if they really knew what they lose when the foreskin is destroyed by this barbaric and inhuman operation . . . .

The pain mentioned by F.H. is indeed a really heavy handicap to any attempts at sexual relief and satisfaction. As he says, the loss of the foreskin nerves makes longer and more vigorous friction of what is left of the responsive areas of touch necessary. The usual result is the fading of erection due (in my own case) to pain around the corona of the permanently exposed glans (a horrible feeling indeed!) even if it is the soft fingers of a wife doing the manipulation! This means frustration and disappointment for both parties, a very sorry state of married togetherness.

My feeling of despairing inadequcy is definitely shared by millions of other unfortunate victims of this barbaric butchery. I wonder when, IN THE NAME OF HUMANITY, a little compassionate (and sane) thinking will be able to put an end to this brutal and disgusting practice! – F.C.

On the other side is this letter:

As a result of a number of childhood incidents I acquired an acute feeling of inferiority over being uncircumcised which eventually developed into a full blown neurosis resulting in mental difficulties.

Our doctor was very understanding, fortunately, and he arranged for me to have psychiatric treatment under the N.H.S. The specialist told me in the course of treatment that I had made things very much more difficult by not seeking it sooner, and I would urge anyone with a psychological difficulty . . . to seek help before it becomes overwhelming.

I was eventually circumcised as part of the therapy and in my case this has certainly proved beneficial. I feel that had I had the operation before my problem became serious I should never have needed to see a psychiatrist but it may equally be the case, as the psychiatrist claimed, that if I had seen him earlier I would not have needed the circumcision. Given the choice, I should choose the operation.

I could have had the operation under the N.H.S. but this involved my going in to hospital for two or three days. This meant getting involved with a fresh set of people, and the whole thing was embarrassing enough as it was. It also meant an explanation to my employers' medical department as to why I had to go into hospital and the likelihood that it would get around the office. After discussion I decided to have it done privately under a local anaesthetic, which at the most only meant taking a day off. The doctor did it one morning at his surgery. I do not suppose I was there more than an hour altogether and I went straight on to work afterwards. No one apart from the doctors and my wife knew anything about it. I experienced no real discomfort and certainly no more than when I had had to have a whitlow lanced.

My judgment is that, when performed by a competent doctor, circumcision is a very trivial operation, and I should advise men unhappy about their uncircumcised state to lose no time in arranging it. – D.H.

And finally, this one:

There have been many letters in your columns on the subject of circumcision some of which I cannot believe are strictly factual. One of your recent correspondents raises a valid point in favour of the operation which I consider requires more investigation.

He expresses surprise that so few women have given views on the subject and would like statistics showing whether or not the almost universal practice of circumcision of males in the United States has reduced the incidence of cancer of the cervix in married women there.

I understand medical evidence shows that among Hindu women this disease is widespread, Hindus being uncircumcised, whereas in Pakistan, which is a Muslim country whose males are all circumcised as a religious rite, it is practically unknown. Furthermore, cancer of the penis is extremely rare amongst Jews and Muslims, who are all circumcised, whereas among Hindus it accounts for no less than 30 per cent of cancer cases in men.

One wonders when it will be recognised that such a trivial operation as circumcision performed in infancy is a worthwhile precaution against the dread scourge of cancer in men and women. On the day medical research shows, without question, that smegma does cause cancer of the cervix in women, our hospitals will be crowded to overflowing with men rushing to be circumcised. This could be avoided if a little commonsense were allowed to prevail. – E.D.

I have come to the conclusion that, with the exception of the clitoral versus the vaginal orgasm controversy, there is no subject in the field of sex more controversial than circumcision. The letters I have just quoted are typical of the arguments which are put forward by both sides, and so are the emotions involved.

Why is it that the retention or removal of a small piece of skin should be so contentious? Why do some men who have been circumcised as children in later life regard themselves as having been mutilated, why others, who have not been circumcised, get into such a psychological state about it that their doctors recommend the simple operation on psychological grounds when no physical grounds exist?

The medical profession gives no guidance, for the division of opinion is as wide between doctors as it is among the lay public. Fortunate are those whose religions – the Jews, the Muslims and various other sects – require all males to be circumcised as a religious rite: at least their minds are made up for them, and I have yet to encounter a Jew or a Muslim who regards himself as having been mutilated, or who has worked himself into an emotional state when involved in the argument. In fact, I have known none who consider that an argument exists.

At the present time the contrast in the general attitudes among those whose religion does *not* require circumcision is well defined in the common practice in Great Britain and the United States. In North America, that is, including Canada, eighty per cent of all males are routinely circumcised before mother and baby are discharged from the maternity hospital, while in Great Britain, unless the parents specifically ask for the operation to be performed, it is unlikely to be, except in those cases where a malformed foreskin is likely to cause dysfunction of the genito-urinary apparatus. Even among those parents who ask for the operation to be carried out, a large proportion meet with resistance from their doctors, who refuse to meet their wishes.

Both in Great Britain and in the United States to circumcise or not to circumcise has gone in cycles. What I mean is that circumcision has been 'in the fashion' in some periods, 'out of fashion' in others. On both sides of the Atlantic during the first four decades of this century, circumcision in infancy, usually within a short time of birth, was widespread among the upper and professional classes. The Second World War, however, had a very pronounced effect on the performance of the operation both here and across the ocean. Because of the medical requirements of the vast armies which both Great Britain and the United States put into the field, there was a shortage of doctors to attend the civilian populations. This shortage led to a review of medical procedures. Applied to circumcision it was found that healthy babies could be circumcised *immediately* after birth with a quicker healing of the wound, fewer subsequent complications and with no shock symptoms; in other words, with complete safety. This policy was adopted in America. In Great Britain, on the other hand, because of the constant risk of air-raids interrupting operations and because of the lower level of medical sterility that was inevitable in partially damaged hospitals, the tendency was to eliminate all absolutely non-essential surgical procedures. Except in those cases where circumcision was deemed to be a medical necessity, it was rarely carried out at all.

After the end of hostilities, a fresh look at circumcision of the newborn was taken in the light of wartime experience, and two clinical studies were made. The conclusions drawn from these studies were diametrically opposed. The main reason for non-religious infant circumcision was a foreskin that would not pull back – or, as the doctors call it, retract. In Great Britain, Professor Douglas Gairdner was able to show that the non-retractable foreskin was a normal condition in newly born babies. As between 16 and 20 babies were dying every year as a direct result of circumcision and as there were numerous cases of post-operation complications, Gairdner decided that the possible benefits of circumcision, which I will describe presently, were not so great as to warrant risking the deaths of a score of babies. He was supported in this view by the great majority of doctors in this country with the result that infant circumcision became virtually unknown except in very special cases, or when the parents insisted, for their own reasons, and were able to find a doctor prepared to operate.

The exactly opposite view was adopted in America based on the study of Professor Harold Speert of New York. He investigated half a million circumcisions over ten years, and found that there had been only one death, and scarcely any post-operative complications. (No one has yet explained why this simple operation carried out by British doctors has a higher death-risk than when performed by American doctors.) Because of the almost one hundred per cent safety of the operation, Speert advocated that circumcision at birth should be routinely carried out on all male babies except in those cases when the parents had conscientious objections. The benefits made such a routine practice well worth while.

So we have the situation today that in America over 90 per cent of all males are circumcised before they leave the maternity hospital, whereas in Great Britain it is rarely performed at all.

Well, what are the benefits of circumcision?

Unfortunately, insofar as the most important benefits are concerned, we can rely only on circumstantial evidence. On the other hand, the weight of this evidence is so considerable that I, personally, do not see how it can be ignored.

First, men who are circumcised in infancy very, very rarely get cancer of the penis. The number of circumcised men who do get this dread disease, which at best means amputation of a large portion of the penis and eventual death, is so small that it is scarcely computable. In Great Britain around 160 men die of it every year.

Second, the number of circumcised men who get cancer of the prostate is considerably lower than the number of uncircumcised men who do.

Third, the wives of circumcised men rarely contract cancer of the cervix.

Benefits two and three are subject to argument, but the many studies carried out into both diseases, and particularly cancer of the cervix, have all reached the conclusion that there must be a strong connection between the disease and the presence or absence of a foreskin, with associate factors in connection with the presence of the foreskin. The chief evidence in connection with cervical cancer is that Jewish women are almost totally immune to it, and though to a somewhat lesser degree, so are Moslem women.

Those who favour the theory of the connection between foreskin and cervical cancer and foreskin and prostatic cancer, suspect – no proof has yet been educed – that what causes the cancer is smegma. There is always a slight seepage of fluid from the penis, and when the man is uncircumcised and wears his foreskin unretracted – as most uncircumcised men do – this fluid is spread over the penis-head and eventually accumulates under the rim. There it solidifies into a soft, whitish, pungently smelling, cheese-like substance, which, if not removed, heightens the irritation of the penis which the collection under the foreskin of grit and fluff from clothes, invariably sets up. This substance is smegma. It makes an early appearance in childhood in some cases, but almost universally at puberty, and continues throughout adulthood. In adolescence it can be equally responsible for encouraging masturbation and the sex-drive and mental and visual stimulation.

It is the presence of smegma that makes male genital hygiene an ABSOLUTE MUST, for apart from its irritative powers (and its suspected connection with cancer) if it is not removed it eventually sets up a disagreeable genital odour which is often so strong that it is detectable at some feet from men so afflicted.

EVERY UNCIRCUMCISED MALE SHOULD BE TAUGHT, FROM EARLY CHILDHOOD, TO PULL BACK HIS FORESKIN AS FAR AS IT WILL GO AT LEAST ONCE A DAY, AND PREFERABLY TWICE, AND WASH THE PENIS WELL WITH SOAP AND WARM WATER, PAYING PARTICULAR ATTENTION TO UNDER THE RIM, SO THAT SMEGMA NEVER HAS TIME TO FORM.

Though smegma is unknown among circumcised men, this practice of daily genital hygiene should be carried out by them as well. Ideally, no man should ever embark on a session of lovemaking without washing his penis, especially if he expects his partner to fellate him.

Unfortunately, the north European, in contrast to the southern European, does not pay sufficient attention to genital hygiene; and more unfortunately still, the Englishman is about the worst offender in this respect, especially if he is working-class. It is a well-known fact that the great majority of Englishmen never wash their penis except when they take a bath, and even then it is quite astonishing how many uncircumcised men do not fully retract their foreskins even in the bath. The middle-classes are just as indolent in this respect. I recently asked fifty boys at a famous public school how often they washed their penises. Only four did so as a part of their regular morning ablutions; the remainder did so only when they bathed, which they did twice a week, though fifteen of the older boys said they usually did – but not always – when taking a shower after a game.

The Ministry of Health ought to launch a public campaign to keep the need for genital hygiene – it applies to women as well – constantly before the public. The Ministry of Education should require all schools, colleges and universities to give special instruction in the subject at regular intervals so that by the time working adulthood is reached genital hygiene has become by nature a daily observance.

Another benefit derived from circumcision is the elimination of such complaints as phimosis, paraphimosis, venereal thrush, balanitis and other conditions involving the foreskin. Phimosis is present when the foreskin is so long and the opening so narrow that the foreskin cannot be pulled back. Since the penis-head can never be cleansed all kinds of irritations and inflammations can result, while in many cases there are adhesions of the foreskin and penis-head which can be extremely painful. Paraphimosis occurs when the unretractable foreskin is suddenly, by some violent movement during masturbation or lovemaking, forced back behind the rim and is so tight that it cannot be pulled forward, even when the penis goes limp. The effect is a strangulated penis, a very painful condition which prevents the circulation of the blood to the penis-head. *Immediate* circumcision is the only remedy. Balanitis and venereal thrush are inflammatory conditions of the foreskin and penis-head which can be quite unpleasant.

On the other hand, those who are against circumcision of the newborn can justifiably point to certain drawbacks to which the circumcised infant can be susceptible. Apart from the fact that there is very rarely an anatomical necessity for the operation to be carried out at birth, and that only a minority will later need the operation for anatomical reasons, there is an infinitesimal element of risk in the operation itself – as I have said, between 16 and 20 babies die in Great Britain as a direct result of the operation every year – and a number (but, again, not a significant number) develop such complications as excessive bleeding or an ulcer on the opening of the penis.

I have said that there is very rarely an anatomical necessity for a newborn child to be circumcised, and some of my readers may wonder why. Well, for quite a number of years after birth – indeed, into adulthood – the foreskin undergoes development and changes. It is first discernible in the embryo at about eight weeks, when it appears as a ring of skin at the base of the penis-head. Thereafter, this ring of skin gradually grows up the penis-head until, by the time the baby is born, the whole penis head is covered by it. At one stage – about the sixteenth week – the surfaces adjoining the foreskin become fused, but thereafter gradually begin to separate. However, though at birth, in the vast majority of babies, the tip of the foreskin has separated sufficiently to allow the passing of urine, it cannot be pulled back over the penis-head. In fact, in three out of four babies it is still unretractable at six months, and in one out of ten, at three years.

Some baby-care experts teach that the foreskin should never be retracted forcibly, but should be allowed to develop in its own way until it can be pulled back naturally. Others, however, advise the mother to begin a very gradual retraction after six months, distending the opening very gently and by millimetres at a time, by forcing it back over the penis-head, so that by nine months or a year the whole penis-head is exposed, and the foreskin can slide freely backwards and forwards over it.

As the child grows up, the foreskin continues to change. It does not do so uniformly in all males, and thus one finds a number of different types of adult foreskins. Thus, there is the elongated foreskin which retains the shape of the infant foreskin, protruding some little way beyond the penis tip, but nevertheless able to be pulled back easily to behind the rim. Most men with this kind of foreskin habitually wear it fully forward and pull it back only to wash, or during masturbation or lovemaking.

In other adult men, the foreskin shrinks and in so doing exposes permanently about one half of the penis-head. If it is pulled forward and then released, it will automatically slide back. In others, it shrinks even further, so that the whole penis-head is permanently uncovered. When attempts are made to pull it forward, it will never cover more than half the penis-head. In the fourth, though comparatively much smaller group, the foreskin disappears altogether; a condition often referred to as auto-circumcision.

Why circumcision at all, then, except in those cases of elongated, unretractable foreskins which are giving trouble?

The answer is that so long as there is a vestige of foreskin smegma will collect under the rim. Ideally, circumcision removes the whole of the foreskin so that the rim that the penis-head makes with the shaft is totally free of all overlapping skin. Unfortunately, some circumcisors do not remove the whole foreskin. I was surprised by the illustrations accompanying the article on circumcision in the Hegelers' *ABZ of Love*, which show this kind of circumcision, as though it were the usual or normal practice. Personally, I can see no point in this partial circumcision, since it allows smegma to accumulate, and requires just as careful genital hygiene as the uncircumcised penis.

I think at this point I may declare my own preference and why. I am in favour of circumcision so long as the foreskin is totally removed, and the reasons for my preference are these:

(1) It makes genital hygiene much simpler and more thorough.
(2) I am greatly impressed by the penile, prostatic and cervical cancer evidence.
(3) To my way of thinking the fully circumcised penis is a much more aesthetic appearing object than the uncircumcised.

With regard to this last point, let me explain a little. If we are honest we have to admit that, wonderful organs though they are, the penis and scrotum are unusual looking objects. It seems to me from my observation of many scores of penises that the foreskin which has been allowed to develop on its own, though eventually totally and easily retractable, does have the effect of preventing the penis-head from developing, in quite a large number of cases, so that it never attains properly balanced proportions in relationship with the rest of the penis. Often the head sits on the shaft like a fairly small acorn perched on the end of a thick stick. I have observed many of these, in my view, disproportionate penis-heads on uncircumcised penises, but not one on a circumcised penis. Maybe this is a very personal point of view – this appreciation of the well-proportioned penis – and I am prepared to be told that it is an idiosyncrasy. On the other hand, I know that I share this visual appeal factor, not only with many men friends, but with many women as well.

You will notice that so far I have not mentioned either the psychological aspects of circumcision nor the more controversial physical effects that it is alleged to have on the penis involved in lovemaking. Let's take the psychological and emotional aspects first. F.C.'s letter which I quoted earlier is typical of the emotive response which circumcision can evoke in some, while D.H.'s letter gives another typical reaction of the uncircumcised.

Fortunately, these two differing responses are found only in a very small minority. The great majority of both circumcised and uncircumcised men accept their penises, whether short of a foreskin or not, as a matter of course. It is only when there are other psycho-sexual factors involved that circumcision either becomes a mutilation or an obsessively desirable state. In the case of the 'mutilation' complex, the reactions are fairly readily comprehended, for though all males have a subconscious fear of mutilation – particularly castration – this fear only surfaces when some hesitation in sexual function concentrates the mind on the genitals. On the other hand, there are some cases, though happily not many, of this obsessive fear being kindled by a specific incident. For example, an old-fashioned parent on catching a boy masturbating may exclaim, 'If I catch you doing that again, I'll cut it off!' or 'If you don't stop doing that it will fall off!' or 'If you keep doing that you'll go mad and it will have to be cut off!' while in adulthood, feelings of inadequacy may be rationalised by the man convincing himself that his partner is a kind of sexual vampire intent on sucking him dry sexually, and eventually rendering him impotent by removing his testicles or mutilating his penis. When genitals become a phobic object, feelings of guilt increase in conjunction with a diffuse anxiety which eventually results in the fear of women and the attempted repression of all sexual temptation. In cases when circumcision becomes mutilation, what the man is really saying is that without the protection of the foreskin, his penis is one hundred per cent vulnerable to any attack the woman (any woman, all women) may direct against it.

The case of the uncircumcised developing an obsessive desire to be circumcised is not so readily explained. This obsession affects only a very small minority and in the few cases which I have personally encountered, the man has generally developed a deep conviction that the circumcised penis is a more reliable lovemaking tool than an uncircumcised one, based on the notion – which I will deal with presently – that the circumcised penis-head is less sensitive than the uncircumcised one, and that this lower sensitivity enables the man to hold back his orgasm longer, thus helping him to be a more successful lover. I have met the circumcision obsession, too, in those men who were one of a number of brothers in a family all of whom had been circumcised except him. The real reason for his not being circumcised not having been explained to him, he first of all imagines that he must have all sorts of things wrong with him which have made him different from his brothers, and this eventually develops into the obsessive desire to be circumcised, 'so that he shall be like *all* the others'. He gets it fixed firmly in his mind that the majority of men are circumcised, and though he is aware that there are uncircumcised men, nothing will convince him that they are not a very small minority, all of whom must have some kind of defect – like himself – which has prevented them from being circumcised.

When the circumcised man is troubled by the mutilation complex, unless he can afford the rarely performed and extremely expensive plastic surgery operation by which a 'foreskin' is grafted over the penis-head, his only hope lies in psychotherapy and this may not often work. The uncircumcised man's obsessive desire to lose his foreskin is much more easily appeased; *there is no age at which a man cannot be circumcised.* The simple operation carried out, it is extremely rare for the obsession not to disappear completely.

Insofar as circumcision performed after the age of, say, seven or eight gives rise to emotional disturbance, there is a certain amount of evidence which shows that this can be a definite risk. On the other hand it does seem to depend very much on two factors: the fullest explanation to the boy as to why the operation is necessary coupled with the ability to assure him absolutely that he is not being mutilated in any way, and that there are millions of other men who have lost their foreskins; and that there are no post-operative complications which give rise to a condition so painful that the operation becomes a traumatic experience. This latter unhappily provides just the right conditions for the development of a variety of emotional disturbances which I need not go into here.

Finally, the argument that the loss of the foreskin deprives the vital orgasm-producing nerves in the penis-tip of their sensitivity.

This argument has a two-way effect.

(1) An uncircumcised man believes his orgasm sensations are vastly superior to the circumcised man's. (See F.H.'s letter.)

(2) Conversely, the uncircumcised man believes that if he were circumcised he would be able to hold back his orgasm longer and so be more successful as a lover.

(3) The circumcised man believes that his less sensitive penis-tip nerves make him a superior lover.

(4) Conversely, the circumcised man believes that because of his less sensitive penis-tip nerves he is being deprived of the maximum sensual experience.

There have been cases in which circumcision has been advocated to overcome premature or too rapid ejaculation, and among such cases there have been claims that the operation has had the desired effect. I do not dispute this, but I do not believe that the removal of the foreskin has *of itself* brought about the desired remedy; in my view, the remedy has been due to the psychological response to the operation. (If this is the real cause of the remedy, it is none the worse for that; however premature ejaculation is overcome, that it is overcome is what matters, not how!)

It does appear to be true, from the evidence of men circumcised after they have had sexual experience, that after a time the penis-head does lose some of its sensitivity. However, as far as one can judge the difference in the degree of sensitivity between the uncircumcised and circumcised penis-head is not very great; in practice, so to speak, it has hardly any effect whatsoever on the achievement of orgasm or the orgasmic experience. In other words, taking the general run of men, there is very little difference in the time taken to stimulate the circumcised and the uncircumcised penis to ejaculation, when allowance is made for the psychological factors involved in the various situations and the psychological response of the individuals.

This contention of mine is supported by the survey into premature and too rapid ejaculation carried out by the magazine *Forum*. I quote from the *Forum* report.

Sensitivity of the penis-head

29 of the 65 subjects are circumcised; 36 are not, but all their foreskins retract very easily, and in 6 cases are worn permanently retracted. This seems to indicate that the loss of sensitivity in the circumcised penis-head is little help in preventing or overcoming rapid ejaculation.

	Circumcised	Uncircumcised
Whole head sensitive	15	18
Rim sensitive	15 (9 with whole head)	21 (8 with whole head)
Frenum	17 (6 with whole head; 11 with rim)	13 (7 with whole head; 9 with rim)
Frenum alone	6	1

When one comes to consider it, this lack of difference in sensitivity between the uncircumcised and circumcised penis-head is logical. The proportion of penises that are completely covered by the foreskin, which though retractable is worn permanently forward is comparatively small, since the majority of men seem to prefer to expose the penis-head for long periods at a time. Even taking the naturally developed foreskin a study of 2,500 uncircumcised penises has revealed that less than half (45 per cent) have foreskins that completely cover the head of the relaxed penis, whereas in 32 per cent the foreskin covered only half the head, and in 23 per cent did not cover it at all. I have recently had the kind co-operation of one hundred circumcised men, of whom 27 had foreskins which completely covered the penis-head. Of these 27 only 9 wore their foreskins permanently forward; the remaining 18 deliberately trained their foreskins to remain behind the rim. (It was interesting to note that in these men, who had carried out this retractive training since their late teens, the depth of the rim was pronounced. It looked as though the constant 'hitching' of the bulky foreskin behind the rim, had caused the rim to develop until it was capable of preventing the foreskin from slipping forward.)

What I am getting at is this. The great majority of uncircumcised men either by design or natural development have the penis-tip exposed. The same conditions that are said to desensitise the penis-tip nerves in the circumcised desensitise the same set of nerves in the uncircumcised penises.

These concentrations of nerves in the penis-head may be designated as orgasm-producing nerves; in the frenum, in the tip around the opening and along and under the ridge of the rim. Those in the frenum are unaffected by circumcision; as I have shown, those in the penis-tip are not all that greatly affected by circumcision, since so many uncircumcised men more or less permanently expose their penis-tips. The only possible difference, therefore, lies in the nerves in the rim, and, as far as my own studies are concerned, these nerves contribute the minimum of sensations in the achievement of orgasm.

To sum up: Except in a small percentage of cases, there is little to choose between the sensitivity of the uncircumcised and the circumcised penis-head.

So I come back to my own preference for circumcision.

(a) I am impressed by the evidence that it seems to have a definite effect on the incidence of penile and prostatic cancer in the man.

(b) I am impressed by the evidence that it seems to have a definite effect on the incidence of cervical cancer in women.

(c) The circumcised penis is much more easily cleaned than the uncircumcised.

(d) The circumcised penis is, to my way of thinking, much more handsome than the uncircumcised penis. If you are susceptible to visual stimulation, this is a very valid consideration.

CHAPTER 6

'I Can't Bring My Wife Off'

Dear Dr Chartham, It doesn't matter what I do, I just can't bring my wife off when we're making love. Yet she has no trouble bringing herself off, which she does in a rather funny way – at least, I think it's funny! She just lies on her side and squeezes her thighs together really hard. What's more, this is the only way she can bring herself off. Not even my attempts at cunnilingus, however long I keep it up, leave her quite unmoved. I find it very difficult to accept the situation in which I find myself. Somehow I feel I am quite inadequate as a lover, and yet whenever I went to bed with a girl, before I got married, of course, I can't remember one who didn't come during coupling. I feel it wouldn't be quite so bad if *I* could bring my wife off either before or after I've gone into her. But the fact that whatever I do – and, believe me, I've reviewed and reviewed and reviewed my techniques, and done everything, but everything, you've suggested in your books – I still can't bring her off and she has to finish herself off, excludes me absolutely from our lovemaking. In my glummest moments I wonder why on earth we go on living together. If she is like this with all men, what it amounts to is that she doesn't need a man at all! Having got so far I wonder why on earth I'm writing and bothering you. At the same time, though, I know why I am – I love her. Can you work a miracle? Can you wave your wand

and make it possible for *me* to satisfy her, either with my finger, mouth or cock? Of course you can't! I know that. But, please can you tell me anything about female frigidity that might, just might, help me to understand? – A.J.

First of all, let us get our terms right. A.J.'s wife is *not* frigid.

There is a good deal of confusion in the lay mind about what true frigidity really entails. A woman is truly frigid when not only does she never reach orgasm, and never has, but has no sexual desire, no sex-drive, no urge whatsoever to make love. The truly frigid woman actively drives off any sexual approach that may be made to her, and if any attempt were made to make love to her, her would-be partner might find that he was actually unable to get his penis into her vagina.

True frigidity is fortunately very rare. It corresponds to full impotence in men, i.e. the inability to get an erection of any kind. Though there are some cases in which frigidity has organic causes, as with male impotence, the majority of cases of true frigidity have psychological causes. Where the cause is organic – and among such causes are inborn defects of the sexual apparatus, or injuries sustained by the sexual apparatus, infection or inflammation of the clitoris, of the neck of the womb, of the ovaries or of the areas surrounding these organs; serious nutritional deficiencies; lesions and defects of the central nervous system and defects in circulation; some diseases such as diabetes, anaemia and leukaemia; and over-indulgence in alcohol and drugs – as I say, where the cause is organic, except when the condition is really serious, there is a possibility of remedy. But such cases, I repeat, are rare.

There are, however, two organic causes which are more common than many people realise and that far too few doctors recognise. The first is connected with hormone production, and with the production of the male hormone testosterone specifically.

Besides producing their male sex hormones, men also produce a small amount of female sex hormones; and similarly women produce a small amount of the male sex hormone, testosterone. Now it is testosterone which activates and regulates sexual desire in *both men and women;* in other words, testosterone produces the sex-drive. Because the amount of testosterone secreted by the woman is considerably less than that produced by the man, in whom it is responsible not only for sexual desire but for the secondary male sexual characteristics, e.g. hair on the face, chest and belly, the deep voice and the growth of the penis and testicles after puberty until maturity, it often happens that this finely balanced secretion in the woman is just deficient enough not to activate sexual desire. In America, though not here because doctors are of the opinion that not sufficient is yet known about hormone therapy to be absolutely certain of its effects, it is a fairly common procedure to give frigid women with a testosterone deficiency, by mouth or by injection, amounts of the hormone in just sufficient quantities to activate libido. Up to now, it has been found that by the administration of hormones, women who have suffered from true frigidity all their lives do *not* respond to this treatment; on the other hand, women who have developed a loss of desire have had it restored in a most dramatic manner by the administration of testosterone.

The second most common organic cause of frigidity is dyspareunia, or painful intercourse. There are a number of reasons why some women experience pain during coupling which I need not go into here. For some women the swinging of the penis in the vagina can be so painful that they develop a tremendous fear of coupling which can cause another condition known as vaginismus. Vaginismus is a spasm of the sphincter muscle surrounding the vaginal entrance, closing the opening entirely so that the man cannot get his penis into the vagina at all. (Some women suffering from dyspareunia do not react with vaginismus as soon as the penis approaches the vagina, but can accept the penis; however, as soon as the swinging penis causes the pain, the vaginal sphincter closes and clamps down on the penis so strongly that the man cannot withdraw. Couples who find themselves in this embarrassing situation can only separate when they have completely relaxed; often they cannot relax unaided, and have to suffer the further embarrassment of having to be taken to hospital thus trapped, to undergo relaxing treatment. Dyspareunia, by the way, is not the only cause of vaginismus; vaginismus is often the result of psychological fear of one kind or another.) However, in a number of cases, the pain is caused by small lesions of the outer and inner lips, and especially of the vagina, which may escape notice during a routine gynaecological examination. If such lesions are found, they can be easily corrected, and with their disappearance the woman ceases to be frigid.

The important point about all this is that, though it is true that the great majority of cases of frigidity have psychological causes, in all cases of frigidity the first step should be a thorough medical and gynaecological examination to rule out any possible organic cause.

As I have said, cases of true frigidity are very rare, fortunately. Not at all rare, however, are cases of what I call pseudo-frigidity. In pseudo-frigidity the woman experiences sexual desire and responds to it with sexual arousal in varying degrees. But there is one common factor in all cases of pseudo-frigidity – *the woman never reaches orgasm during loveplay with her heterosexual partner*.

As I pointed out in the chapter on male impotence and partial impotence – of which frigidity and pseudo-frigidity are the female counterparts – it is difficult for the layman to appreciate the enormous influence which the mind exerts over our sexual functioning. An almost innumerable variety of psychological reactions can affect our sexual performance. The smallest incident can create such a psychological block that we are prevented absolutely from obtaining the natural conclusion of sexual arousal – relief of tension through orgasm.

The causes of psychologically induced partial impotence in men are numerous enough, but the psychological causes of pseudo-frigidity are even more so. They fall, on the whole, into two chief categories – those which have the relationship with the husband or partner as their mainspring, and those which have a wide spectrum of non-relationship bases.

Let us take the relationship causes first. It will be difficult for many women reading this to accept much of what I shall say, simply because they are totally unconscious of the reason, and because, when it is pointed out to them, it is so contrary to their conscious attitude towards the partner that it seems laughable.

Vera B had been happily married, so she claimed, to her husband, Richard, for three years. During all that time, she had experienced orgasm during lovemaking only during the first six months or so. She was twenty-seven when she became Richard's wife, and had given up a very responsible and lucrative post as personal assistant to the managing director of a large industrial concern to marry. She and Richard had made love half a dozen times or so before they married, and had never failed to enjoy the experience and reach a climax.

'Looking back,' she told me, 'it was good fun during the first few months we were married, but gradually I became conscious of my desire getting less and less, and my ability to come off correspondingly impaired. By the end of eight months, whatever Richard did during loveplay, though I used to respond physically to his stimulation I had little or no arousal sensations, and even if he prolonged loveplay for an hour or more, orgasm was never in sight. I love him, and in all other aspects of our life together, we were happy. Recently, though, I've sensed that Richard is beginning to lose interest. I wouldn't blame him if he were. I have a suspicion that he's got another girl-friend, and it's because

I still care for him enough not to want to share him that I've come to you.'

'Why have you waited so long?' I asked her.

'Well, after about a year with nothing happening we did go to see our G.P. I suggested it, because Richard was getting into such a state. He blamed himself, said he was a failure as a lover, and was becoming so frustrated that his temper was suffering terribly, and we nearly always finished our lovemaking with a row. The doctor told us that what was happening to me happened to a lot of women, and that everything would be all right after we'd had a baby. So we had Mark, but everything isn't all right. In fact, things are getting worse.'

It was these last few sentences that gave me the clue.

'How are you coping with the baby?' I asked.

She looked at me puzzled, and said just a little bit aggressively, 'Quite well. Why do you ask?'

'I wondered whether you might be finding having to devote so much of your time to him a bit of a chore.'

'Oh, I see,' she replied. 'Well, he does make quite a bit of extra work, naturally, but I've always found house-keeping rather frustrating, I'm afraid.'

Now I was sure I was on the right track. Vera's trouble in reaching orgasm during lovemaking with Richard, I believed, had its origins in the fact that Richard had insisted that she should give up her job when they got married. When I put it to her that she missed her work and would be delighted to go back to it, she was honest enough to admit it straight away. She was naturally some-what startled when I suggested that she was resentful towards Richard for depriving her of her career, and she resisted at first. But as we talked I managed to show her that what I was suggesting was fact. Not only was she resentful towards Richard for depriving her of her career, her resentment was also fanned by the success Richard was so obviously making of his own career. The extra work the baby made only served to accentuate the resentment.

(The G.P. had rather jumped to conclusions. While there are quite a number of women who do not experience orgasm during lovemaking with their husbands until they have had a baby, in the majority of such cases the psychological cause of their pseudo-frigidity is the fear that childbirth will be excessively painful. They have probably listened to the highly-coloured accounts of the experiences in the labour-room of older married sisters or sisters' friends, who have exaggerated their experiences to attract special attention. Once these women discover for themselves that childbirth today is not painful, the fear disappears and they have no further motive for trying to reject sex – which they have been doing in the past by withholding orgasm – and for the first time in their married lives they are able to enjoy lovemaking because the baby they are suckling at the breast emerged without any undue difficulty.)

Vera found it very hard to believe that unconsciously she was deliberately withholding her orgasm in order to punish Richard for depriving her of her career, but she was an intelligent girl and eventually was able to accept my diagnosis. The difficulty remained, nevertheless, in finding a practical solution to her problem, because very often though the psychological block may be uncovered, the recognition of it does not necessarily make the difficulty magically disappear. The baby Mark, of course, complicated matters because he was so young. She could not take a job outside the home immediately, but I thought it might go some way towards a solution if Richard would agree that as soon as their domestic circumstances permitted he would not object to Vera taking a job. (He had vetoed her carrying on with her job after marriage because he believed in the rather old-fashioned idea that a husband should be able to support his wife without her having to work. He admitted this and added that his business colleagues might think he could not afford to support her himself; in other words, that he was not being all that successful. But he was now so patently successful, that no one would believe he could not support his family, and he was able to accept this point.)

Well, he agreed that Vera should have a job, and though she knew that it would not be for a year or two, she could accept the promise he had given her. I had not expected Vera to have an orgasm the first time they made love; I thought it might take a little time for her to get used to their new understanding. It was obvious, however, that though she had unconsciously resented him so bitterly, she had been telling the truth when she had told me she loved him.

Sorting out the problem had been a bit wearing all round, so I suggested that if possible they should park Mark with one of his grandmothers for a couple of nights, and that they should go off by themselves for a weekend. They were able to arrange it. Early on Monday morning Vera rang me. I could tell from her voice that something had happened.

'It's wonderful,' she said. 'It seems as though we hardly stopped making love all the weekend, and I came every time. I can't tell you how often I came. I don't know now whether I shall ever go back to work, but it makes all the difference knowing that if ever I want to, Richard won't say no.'

I have related this case at length to show how easily unconscious attitudes towards the husband-wife relationship can affect the physical sexual functioning quite drastically. Resentment against the partner is only one of the causes of psychologically induced sexual dysfunction. Other causes quite often encountered are perhaps a little easier to understand.

A woman may feel, after she has been married for a few months, that her husband does not really love her, or she may discover that she does not really love him as she believed she did. Or she may get the idea that he wants to fuck her too often, that he is not really expressing his love through his lovemaking, but is using her body merely as a means of getting relief from sexual tension, despite the fact that he takes his time over his lovemaking and has acquired quite skilful techniques. She may discover that he has various little habits which were not revealed while they were courting which she finds excessively irritating, and though they may be quite small idiosyncrasies, they are enough to make him less physically attractive than he was in the first place.

One young woman came to me not long ago who had been brought up in a sexually liberal family. She had seen both parents and her two older brothers naked from childhood until she left home at twenty. She had even had two reasonably satisfactory love affairs.

I was to discover that by coincidence her father, brothers and two lovers had all been circumcised. Her husband, with whom she did not make love and whom she did not see naked until after they were married, was not circumcised, and in addition had a very long foreskin, which he habitually wore forward, though it retracted quite easily. She found the appearance of his penis so physically unaesthetic that she had difficulty in accepting what she called 'that deformed thing' in her vagina, and although she did overcome her revulsion sufficiently to let him put it into her, all the time they were coupling she visualised it moving backwards and forwards inside her. 'I just can't help it,' she told me. 'I know I am being absolutely unreasonable, but I can't let myself go. He tries every way he can think of to bring me off, but I can't come. I either have to finish off myself, or let him do it for me after he's come and lost his erection. I can't even come if he stimulates me orally, if I know he's got an erection. What can we do?'

'Do you think he would agree to be circumcised?' I suggested.

'I don't know. But would it work?'

'I can't be absolutely certain,' I told her, 'but I think it would be worth trying.'

When I explained the position to the husband, he readily agreed to be circumcised, and happily it worked. The first time they were able to make love after the operation, she had not one, but three orgasms. She does not know it, but I don't think she will ever be able to make love satisfactorily with an uncircumcised man.

Many of the psychological causes of the woman being unable to reach orgasm during coupling have no connection with the partner. Women who have been brought up in a puritan atmosphere and have been taught, or at least given to understand that sex is a disgusting subject, almost invariably develop pseudo-frigidity after marriage. This is particularly true where the mother has herself developed a deep-rooted dislike, even hatred, of all sexual activity. The condition in such cases is quite a severe one because she cannot accept freely the loveplay caresses of her husband, let alone his coupling with her. In fact, she rarely achieves sexual release at all, except possibly through erotic dreams, because she is inhibited from bringing herself off and finds her husband's finger stimulation of the clitoris and his oral stimulation of her nipples equally produce no response, because her own sex organs are as disgusting to her as her husband's erect penis is.

Fear of pregnancy – not of childbirth, but of producing an unwanted child – is a very common cause of pseudo-frigidity. Women who have this fear nearly always respond well to self-stimulation, and even more readily to their partner's direct stimulation of the clitoral and vaginal areas, especially to cunnilingus. But as soon as the penis is put into the vagina they 'freeze up', and no amount of pelvic and penile swinging will produce any sensation. Usually the pseudo-frigidity is removed if great care is taken to provide the woman with a really safe method of contraception, particularly The Pill and the IUD, or better still, if the husband is sterilised. My first wife never came off during coupling until we agreed that I should have a vasectomy after the birth of our second child, entirely because I was a very poor university professor, able to support two children only with difficulty, and we saw no prospect of my being able to earn more. With the fear of pregnancy removed completely, she was transformed overnight. Before she had often teased me about being sex-mad; now there were very frequent occasions when I found it difficult, though pleasantly so, to meet her requirements.

This fear of pregnancy which has prevented the woman from coming during love-making all her life is, of course, removed by the menopause, and this is the reason why many women in their later fifties suddenly seem to become extremely sexy and readily responsive. Even women who have been able to reach orgasm regularly may find their sexual desire become more urgent and their sexual responsiveness more intense after the menopause. merely because the fear of unwanted pregnancy has been removed.

Some women who experience strong sexual desire and intense orgasms, and can easily reach climax when they masturbate themselves, are unable to come off either with finger or oral stimulation by their partners, or by penis-vagina contact. Conscious of their strong sexuality they are afraid that if they really let themselves go while making love, they will shock their partner. If only they knew how much most normal, average men appreciate and get an extra thrill out of making love to a really sexy, uninhibited woman! Men who have this good fortune are more apt to congratulate themselves on their own prowess as a lover, who is able to make a woman respond so intensely, than to attribute the woman's response to her sexuality.

Girls who in their teens have formed strong emotional attachments with their fathers, and particularly those who have had recognisable incestuous desires, are very often incapable of coming off when made love to by any other man. In such case it is usually the unconscious feeling of guilt at betraying the father that sets up the block. And there are girls who are so keen on providing their own sexual pleasure that they cannot co-operate with another human being, man or woman, even when that co-operation could lead to sexual pleasure for them.

But probably the greatest cause of pseudo-frigidity is the legacy of shame and guilt which, despite the more generally liberal attitudes towards sex and sexual behaviour, still, surprisingly, operate in relation to sex in so many people's minds. Nowadays it is not so much guilt, though very many women do have strong guilt feelings in relation to sex, as intense shame. This shame is somewhat different from guilt. When one feels guilty about something, it is generally because that 'something' is contrary to religious or moral teaching. When we transgress religious or moral teaching we feel we have been wicked, and because we have been wicked we feel guilty that we have not been able to control our actions sufficiently by moral strength or religious precept.

Shame, on the other hand, does not result from transgressing either moral or religious precepts, and though religious and moralistic transgression is to a degree a personal thing, shame is intensely personal because it springs from feelings of inadequacy. Inadequacy in the sexual sphere is, by any standard, much more devastating to self-respect than guilt can ever be. It means more to the man, in our present climate, than it does to the woman simply because he has taken too much to heart the pernicious teaching of Dr Marie Stopes that unless he can bring off his partner *every* time they make love, he is a failure as a lover. In the past, a man measured his sexual self-esteem by the ease with which he could produce an erection, the strength of the erection and his fertility index. Nowadays, although he sets prime store on his erection, he regards his cock and its rigidity chiefly as the member through which he expresses his sexual adequacy.

Adequacy in relation to sexual behaviour and activity is a comparatively recent concept. It has its origins, of course, in the Stopean concept, which I have just quoted.

This concept of sexual inadequacy in its application to both sexes has tended to replace to a large extent the guilt which the transgression of religious and moral sex laws promoted, by shame. Though good old-fashioned guilt, which induces feelings of sinfulness, still has an influence on sexual behaviour and performance, the shame which sexual inadaquacy produces is an even more potent factor in our practical sex-lives. As the influence of religion dwindles and sexual morality becomes adjusted to our new attitudes towards sexual behaviour, so sexual shame will become more and more predominant, and the sexual inadequacy from which it derives will play an even more prominent role in our sex-lives. While in *all* we do we measure our worthiness not by how morally or religiously good we are, but by the success we achieve in the various compartments of our lives, so shame and its twin, sexual inadequacy, will dominate our emotional and physical expression of sex.

Shame and sexual inadequacy have already invaded the realms of, and are strongly influencing, the woman's response to sex to an almost comparative extent that they regulate the man's sexual responsiveness. Where the man defines adequacy as the capacity to obtain a potent erection and sustain it long enough to allow the slower woman to achieve orgasm, the woman defines adequacy, not in terms of tumescence – the swelling of her vaginal lips and the erection of nipples and clitoris – and time, but by her ability to reach climax at all. The pseudo-frigid woman is now regarded as sexually inadequate as the impotent or partially impotent man, and not by the man only, but by her herself. Though I do receive a number of letters from men complaining of their partner's pseudo-frigidity, I receive far more letters from women themselves asking how they can achieve orgasm. And it is significant, I think, that when it is the men who are complaining, they nearly always do so in the terms that A.J. has used in the letter with which I started this chapter, '*I* can't bring my wife off.' *Not,* my wife can't come off whatever *I* do, but *I* can't bring her off whatever *I* do. The man is still equating his partner's lack of orgasmic response with his own sexual prowess; in other words, he is blaming his own sexual inadequacy for her lack of orgasmic ability. And this wrong assessment is creating greatly enhanced sex difficulties for it produces a couple of sexually inadequate individuals where there need be only one.

How then should a man react to his partner's pseudo-frigidity?

Well, now, recently I have been carrying out an investigation into the sex-drive and the lovemaking techniques of couples in their middle-twenties, thirties and early forties. One of the questions I asked was, 'Who decides when you shall couple? The man or the woman?' I have been horrified to discover that more men than women decide when the penis shall be put into the vagina, and that none of these men ask the woman if she is ready for the final phase of lovemaking.

This discovery has shocked me, *because penis-vagina contact should not usually be made until the woman has been roused to the threshold of the point-of-no-return,* and NO MAN CAN POSSIBLY KNOW OR JUDGE WHEN THE WOMAN HAS REACHED THIS VITAL POINT ON HIS OWN; THE WOMAN MUST TELL HIM SHE WANTS THE PENIS IN HER.

Having made this discovery, I have now made it a rule when trying to advise in cases of frigidity, and especially in those cases where the woman can be brought off by finger or oral stimulation of the clitoris, to ask these questions first of all.

(1) Who decides when the penis is put into the vagina?
(2) When this is decided, does the woman feel that she is at the threshold of the point-of-no-return? In other words, would she come off within *seconds* if the loveplay stimulation were continued?

I find that if the answer to question 1 is *the man,* the answer yo question 2 is almost invariably, 'I would like stimulation to continue a little longer.' In these cases I tell the couple that the woman is not pseudo-frigid at all, but the victim of a poor loveplay technique. I stress that the man must *not* put his penis into the vagina until the woman indicates she is ready, and that the woman must not give this indication until she is actually about to come off.

Nor is it simply a matter of the man getting his penis into the vagina. Whatever position is being used, the penis must be inserted with the least possible delay. This is made necessary by the fact that the woman's arousal sensations fall off very rapidly once loveplay clitoral stimulation stops, and if there is a longish delay while the man fumbles about trying to get his cock in the right place, by the time he is in she may have fallen right back to the beginning arousal-wise. Then, unless he can keep his swinging movement going for twenty minutes or more without coming, he will never be able to bring her off.

As soon as the decision to couple has been taken, the woman should immediately reach down with both hands, draw the vaginal lips apart with two or three fingers, and with a finger of each hand should guide the penis to the vagina entrance. (In the rear-entry positions, of course, the man is so poised that he can guide his penis to the vagina entrance himself.) If by the time the cock has got in place the woman's sensations have receded considerably, it is *absolutely essential* that *she should tell her partner,* and he must then apply finger-clitoral stimulation while still coupled, until she reaches the point-of-no-return again. Personally, I think it should be a rule that whenever a position for coupling allows easy access to the clitoris, the man should always continue finger-clitoral stimulation even if the woman is very highly roused when they couple. She can be brought to multiple orgasm in this way, for, except in a small number of women, the clitoris, unlike the penis-tip, does not become excessively sensitive to touch.

I have also had cases which have proved to be not

pseudo-frigidity but just sheer bad loveplay techniques on the man's part. In such cases the woman nearly always complains that she takes a very long time to come off, even though her partner is a skilful lover. More often than not, she has no standard by which to judge whether or not he is a skilful lover. Because he has a variety of caresses, can hold back his own progress towards orgasm for a long time and does not hurry over foreplay, she decides he must be a skilful lover. Unfortunately, he – also almost invariably – regards himself as a skilful lover.

In point of fact, he may be actually an unskilful lover, despite his knowing the sensitive zones which produce sexual arousal when caressed, and does indeed caress them. I have said this before many times, but I must say it again: It is all very well for people like myself to describe the sensitive zones and the caresses to which they respond, but unless everyone reading us realises that we are merely making general observations and giving general indications, no one is going to get the maximum benefit from following our directions. What we must drum home again and again is the fact that sexually each of us is an individual. We may respond to caresses of the generally recognised sensitive zones, but nearly every single one of us has a personal sensitive zone to which we respond more intensely than to our general sensitive zones, or alternatively, one special kind of caress in one of the general sensitive zones may call forth a highly intense response, or we may respond most intensely to a special caress in our personal sensitive zone.

But whatever our preferences are, our partners are most unlikely to discover them of their own accord, however skilful lovers they may be. *We have to tell them what we want them to do precisely, and precisely where.* As in all other aspects of sex, to be really completely successful lovers *we must communicate* about practical matters like caresses.

Quite a number of partners of pseudo-frigid women write to ask if masturbation can be the cause. They have the notion that women can do themselves some physical harm by masturbating. (Many men have the same fear about their own masturbation.) Let me give an absolute categorical assurance that it is impossible for either men or women to harm themselves physically by masturbation, even if they masturbate a dozen times a day.

On the other hand, in rare cases a masturbatory technique can cause pseudo-frigidity. This is what has happened with A.J.'s wife. (The letter I quoted at the beginning.) But, don't misunderstand me. It is not the physical technique that is causing the trouble. Though A.J. finds it a peculiar technique, masturbation by squeezing the thighs together is fairly common among women masturbators.

The influence of masturbation on Mrs A.J.'s pseudo-frigidity is, in fact, psychological. What A.J. did not put in his letter – because he did not know – was that when Mrs A.J. masturbates she can only reach orgasm if she relives the experience of her first masturbation. From her bedroom window she overlooked the bathroom, and one day in summer her elder brother, on coming in from tennis, went for a shower. The bathroom window was open, and probably not realising that he could be seen he did not close it. Quite by chance she was sitting by the window of her bedroom, sewing, and the movement in the bathroom caught her attention.

She had not seen her brother naked since he was twelve or so, and had never seen a penis in the flesh before. Fascinated, she watched him drying himself. When he had finished drying, he began to stimulate himself, and more fascinated than ever, she could not take her eyes from him. Though she did not know what he was doing, she became aware that she was strangely excited, and as his hand moved faster over his penis, she squeezed her thighs together, and presently became conscious of extraordinary sensations, which she had not experienced before, and which mounted to a climax, leaving her flushed and breathless.

That night in bed, she visualised the bathroom scene

again, and as she did so realised that she was squeezing
her thighs together and was inducing the same sensations
she had experienced before. The following morning before
she got up, she repeated the process, doing so several times
a day over the next week or two. Every time she visualised
her brother masturbating, and when she tried later to
masturbate without the aid of the visualisation, she found
that no matter how tightly she squeezed her thighs together,
she could not induce the orgasm sensations, let alone reach
climax. So each time she masturbated she had to project
the picture of her brother in her mind.

When she did learn that what she was doing was masturbating, and that other girls did so by stimulating the clitoris
with a finger, she attempted that method. She found,
however, that no matter how long she stimulated herself
in that way, she could not reach orgasm. In fact, the only
way she could bring herself off was by squeezing her thighs
together and visualising her brother masturbating. For
nearly twenty years this has been the only way in which
she has been able to get relief from her sexual tension. For
her purposes her brother has ceased to be her brother and
has become a good looking seventeen-year-old boy. Never
once has she achieved orgasm with a penis in the vagina,
or, for that matter, by any stimulation technique any
partner has applied to her.

She came to me because psychotherapy had failed,
chiefly because she took an instant dislike to the analyst.
For some months she had been making love with a man of
her own age, for whom she had developed sincere feelings
of love. This was probably the first time in her life that she
had genuinely and whole-heartedly fallen in love, and yet
she could not come off during their lovemaking, despite
the fact that he really was an experienced and skilful lover.
She was also intelligent enough to realise that if her lover
discovered that he was not bringing her off, it would
upset him very much, and she was afraid it might affect
his responses to their fucking, landing him with a

psychological block, too. She had simulated orgasm successfully so far, but was anxious lest one day he would find out
that she never came off; and in any case, she desperately
wanted to come while they were coupled.

I suggested that she ought to undergo another course
of psychotherapy, but this time making sure, before she
began the treatment, that she was *en rapport* with the analyst.
She was not very keen on this, because of her previous
experience, and asked me if I could not think of some way
of getting her to function normally.

(Psychotherapy is the recognised treatment for removing
psychological blocks which inhibit normal sexual functioning. I am not a trained psychiatrist, though as a counsellor
I have to have quite a deep understanding of human
psychology. In a number of cases where psychotherapy
has failed I have found that a suggestion of practical
application succeeds. It is absolutely essential that the
vicious circle in which most psychological blocks affecting
sexual function revolve should be broken. Sometimes if
the circle can be broken just once, everything thence-
forward operates normally; but in other cases it may be a
little time before this happens, and so patience on the part
of the 'patient' and adviser is a first requirement.)

As I saw this particular case, the young woman had two
psychological blocks which had to be removed: one, her
inability to reach orgasm by any other method of masturbation except by squeezing her thighs together; two, her
inability to reach orgasm except by masturbation. I
decided to concentrate first on getting her to come off by
some other method of masturbation, and suggested the
use of a vibrator, as there are not many women who do
not respond with orgasm to this method of stimulation.
Even with this she had some difficulty. If her partner used
the vibrator she came off, but if she used it herself, she did
not. As soon as she began to approach climax she would
move the vibrator away. We eventually overcame that
by getting her to hold the vibrator while her hand was held

firmly in place so that she could not take it away when the sensations mounted. Once that was achieved, it was not long before she could masturbate by finger-stimulation of the clitoris. However, she could never come off by any method of masturbation unless she visualised her brother masturbating in the bathroom.

We then went on to try to remove the second block. This proved rather more difficult. A suggestion that after the penis had been put in her she should close her legs and squeeze her thighs together almost did the trick, but not quite. This was largely due to the fact she resisted the idea of fantasising about her brother while being fucked by her lover; a point of view with which I was sympathetic. The only way in which we might succeed, I thought, was if we could somehow substitute the teenage brother – who, since the brother was now over forty and very different from the seventeen-year-old in physique and appearance, was by this time a fantasy figure – by the lover. The only way in which I thought this might be done was if she observed him masturbating in the bathroom in somewhat similar conditions to those under which she had observed her brother masturbating that summer afternoon.

This meant that the co-operation of her lover was necessary, and, as I have said earlier, she had insisted that he should not be told of her difficulty in case it gave him feelings of sexual inadequacy and affect his performance. However, I did eventually manage to persuade her that he could be told without this risk, if she would let me do the telling.

The major obstacle confronting us was to reconstruct as closely as possible the conditions of the original incident. Even if we found a bathroom overlooked by a bedroom window, how on earth were we going to explain matters to the tenant of the house in order to persuade him to let us use it? The problem was insurmountable, it seemed.

It was the lover who solved the problem in the end. He realised that one of the bedrooms in the flat faced the bathroom, and that if both doors were left open anyone in the bedroom could observe what was going on in the bathroom. It seemed worth a try, and to foster the illusion as much as possible he mocked up a 'flat' representing a window in a brick wall, which was placed in the open doorway of the bathroom. I was doubtful whether it would succeed, but fortunately my doubts proved groundless, and she was subsequently able to replace the fantasy brother with the fantasy of the lover, and by visualising the scene of the lover in the bathroom while they are coupling she is able to come off. The only snag that may be involved is that I doubt very much whether she will be able to make love to orgasm now with any man but her lover; but as they are very much in love, I hope this will not have to be put to the test.

Now, this could not have been achieved but for the patience and sympathetic understanding of the partner. Some men would have undoubtedly jibbed at being required to masturbate knowing that they were being observed, even though the voyeuse was the partner. This young man, however, did not hesitate, and it was his ready compliance in my view which was one of the major factors in the success of the undertaking. And this brings me to perhaps the most important thing the partner of a pseudo-frigid woman can do.

He must be prepared to co-operate fully in any programme of treatment advised. He must make sure that he understands fully what the problem is, and he must be patient, sympathetic and encouraging. When the 'patient' wants to give up, he must insist, firmly but kindly, that she does not. He must not expect any miraculously speedy results, and he must be prepared to dispel any depression in the patient that a dishearteningly long period of treatment will undoubtedly cause from time to time. In fact, it is essential that he should understand the importance of his role, which is, put bluntly, that success or failure will largely depend, not on his sexual adequacy, but on his strength as a prop for his partner's sexual inadequacy. He must try to transfer his own sexual confidence to her.

Probably in no case of pseudo-frigidity can he play a more positive part than in those cases where the pseudo-frigidity is caused by an exaggerated interpretation of feminine modesty. A very large number of cases of pseudo-frigidity result from the fact that the woman cannot let herself go sexually because she feels that to do so would make her appear immodest, wanton, unladylike. Because, in the past, women were taught that men were the sexual aggressors to whose demands they had to submit willy-nilly, many conceived the notion that if they showed any interest in sexual activity they would be betraying the traditional feminine role. While content to be used so that their partner could be sexually satisfied, they expected him to treat them with respect, to do nothing which would affront their modesty. Just to have to lie there, to receive his penis and to have him bucking about *on top* of them was affront enough; but to have him fingering, licking or sucking the clitoris, and especially to submit to his demands for fellatio, or to fucking in rear-entry positions was particularly degrading. But though in marital duty bound to submit to such demands, they could retain their self-respect by refusing to co-operate fully, i.e. by letting themselves come off. In other words, they were with-holding themselves from sex – and incidentally from their partners – purely to bolster their exaggerated sense of feminine modesty.

Unfortunately, in spite of the fact that the attitudes towards the woman's role in sex have changed consider-ably, there are still a large number of women (far more, I think, than is generally appreciated) who cling to the old concept of the sexual anaesthetic cunt as the ideal of feminine sexuality. If this were not true, I would not receive the many letters from men that I do complaining that their partners kill the excitement that might be experienced in lovemaking by refusing to co-operate because doing so-and-so 'isn't nice'—in other words, is kinky or perverted.

How often must we stress that there is nothing, absolutely nothing, that a couple can do with one another sexually in the privacy of their home that can be depraved or can degrade either partner if both are willing to participate, and there is no good reason why they should not participate?

Somehow or other, when the woman attempts to operate her sex-life on the basis of exaggerated modesty, the man must find some way of coaxing her out of it. This is not easy, because she must not be *forced* into doing something against her will, for that will only lead to further trouble of functioning. The man will know his partner well enough to know whether a direct approach or a more subtle one will be the best one; in other words, he will either come right out with what he would like them to do, or by slow, subtle suggestion and action on his part, lead her gradually up to it.

Two suggestions that are often found to be effective are these: words written by some stranger and printed in a book are more likely to be accepted by many women than any number of arguments put forward verbally by the partner;* and the use of the persuasive, 'Try it just once, please, just because you love me!' The latter is probably not really sporting, but, in my view, it is quite justifiable since, in my experience at any rate, once it is established that the act, whatever it may be, is pleasurable, the woman wonders why she made all the fuss.

I admit that the man is confronted by quite a task, but patience and cunning, directness or subtlety, according to the psychological make-up of the woman, and above all kindness, can overcome pseudo-frigidity resulting from exaggerated modesty. More difficult, perhaps, is overcoming the pseudo-frigidity caused by the woman's

* I think my chapter on frigidity in the companion book *Advice to Women* could help here.

over-determination to achieve full sexual gratification. Such women are not inhibited by considerations of modesty, nor by a sense of guilt. They are quite prepared to do everything and anything suggested by the partner. Yet they rarely reach orgasm – in some cases never.

It is their over-determination which is preventing them from having a really satisfying climax. Over and over again, I say to women and their partners, 'You are trying too hard. You are getting yourselves worked up into a tizzy about it, when you ought to be relaxing and just letting it happen.' But the difficulty in persuading them that they are failing because they are trying too hard presents quite a challenge, because such women are the victims of our old enemy, shame. They are also the victims of the rat-race, which can, and does, invade the sexual aspects of life as surely as any other aspect of living. They know that the sexually successful woman responds to lovemaking with unfailing climax, sometimes simultaneously with her partner, or, nowadays, with multiple orgasms. She *must* be a sexually successful woman, otherwise she cannot claim to be successful as a woman. (She is like the man who is a failure as a lover unless he can bring off his partner every time they make love.) She does not mind what she has to do to achieve this success, nor how she must act and react so long as she comes off.

It is this 'how' that is her great stumbling-block to achieving the success she is pursuing. When she is making love, she concentrates on *how* she can arouse herself sexually and *how* she can most intensely respond to her partner's arousal techniques. To make things even more complicated, however, this *how*, which, if acted upon at face value, ought to have the desired effect, is, in fact, masking the real motive of all her efforts – 'I must have an orgasm because my best friend Mavis never fails to come off every time', 'I must have as many orgasms as possible, at least as many as Mavis, because I can't think she is a more successful woman than I can be', 'I must make the bells ring and the lights flash when I come off, because Mavis says she always does, and if it happens to Mavis I've got to make it happen to me.'

It scarcely needs me to point out that because her mind – which controls her sexual responses – is clogged with her fierce competition with all the Mavises she knows, it cannot concentrate on providing her with the success she so desperately needs. While lovemaking, the mind should be clear of all other subjects so that it can apply itself as completely as possible to rousing the body to the achievement of the physical ecstasy which is the expression of emotional love, which, in turn, is the main reason for lovemaking.

A little further consideration of this particular situation reveals, of course, that we have once again come up against 'the vicious circle'. The woman who is determined to be successful fails because she concentrates more on avoiding failure than on achieving success. It is the fear of failure that creates the failure.

Here again, the partner, in my view, is the person to overcome this type of induced pseudo-frigidity rather than the psychiatrist. He must convince her that because he loves her she should be wanting to succeed for him rather than wanting to put one over on Mavis. Who the hell cares about how often Mavis comes off, how loudly the bells ring, how brilliantly the lights flash? It is her response to *his* love, which he is trying to express through his physical lovemaking with her, that is the important thing. She should concentrate on making him happy rather than on making Mavis jealous. And what does it matter if she doesn't always come off, so long as she is not left high and wet and so long as she has been happy enough in their lovemaking to show how much she loves him by what she has let him do to and for her and by what she has done to and for him? Coming or not coming is a private matter between partners; there are no competitors.

Finally, then, if a man takes the trouble to acquire the

knowledge of and the mastery over the general techniques of lovemaking, and learns the idiosyncrasies of his partner's body and sexual needs, he should not accuse himself of inadequacy if his partner fails to come off, whatever he does. He must accept the fact that she has her problems; tactfully and kindly he must try to discover what the problems are; and then kindly, patiently and persistently he must do all he can – whether encourage her to undertake psychotherapy, or attempt to remove the blocks himself – to help eliminate the problem.

There are very few pseudo-frigid women who need be pseudo-frigid; there are even fewer who do not respond to the right treatment.

CHAPTER 7

Oral Intercourse

We have been married for six years [a woman has written to me this morning] and have had a satisfying and happy sex-life. I think I may say that I have never refused to do anything sexual my husband has asked me to do. We often make love in the sitting-room, and I get very stimulated watching us doing it in front of a mirror. We've even made love in the bath. So, you see, I'm not really prudish, but now I think I've got to draw the line.

On one or two occasions recently my husband has moved down me during foreplay and tried to caress my clitoris with his mouth and tongue. I haven't let him, of course, because I don't think it's very nice. But he says lots of people do, and the wives suck their husband's penis as well. That really strikes me as perverted. I don't think I could ever do that to him, however much I loved him. What do you think? Is it perverted? Do lots of people do it? What can I do so that I don't make him unhappy?

Then there is this letter from my files.

Dear Mr Chartham, The other night while I and my husband were making love, he began to play with my clitoris with his tongue. It seemed to stimulate him tremendously, because he came off in a short time in my hand, and I have to admit that I found

it very stimulating, too. He has done it on one or two
occasions, but I am worried. Do you think he's
suddenly become kinky? I'm also not sure in my
mind whether I ought to enjoy it like I do. It doesn't
seem natural, really.

Or this one.

Dear Mr Chartham, I have a problem, and I
wonder if you can help me, please. We have been
married seven months. During the year we were
engaged we made love two or three times a week,
but never during that time did my husband, as he
now is, play with my clitoris with his tongue, which
is what he has started to do recently. I have nothing
against him doing it if he wants to and likes it, because
I find it very stimulating. But now he wants me to
suck his penis, and I just can't bring myself to do it.
You see, as soon as his penis becomes erect he starts
to make a lot of lubricating fluid. You say in *Sex
Manners for Men* that this fluid does not taste or
smell, and though I believe you, somehow I have
the idea at the back of my mind that I shall taste it.
And what if he comes in my mouth? If this happened,
I know I should be sick.

And there is this.

My husband wants us to use oral-genital caresses
while we are making love. I am quite prepared to do
this, but I seem to remember reading somewhere
that it can lead to all kinds of diseases because the
genitals have very many germs on and around them.
What do you think?

Every week I get several letters from women along these
lines, and a few from men. The men mostly complain that

their wives refuse to caress their penises with their mouths and ask if I can advise them how to overcome this problem, while some also find that though they would desperately like to be caressed in this way, they also think it is unethical, or immoral, or signifies deviation tendencies. Like the man who wrote:

Dear Mr Chartham, I am writing to you in desperation, and I hope you will be able to help me. When we were making love the other night, my girl-friend began to kiss and suck my penis. What made her do it I don't know. She says she just felt like it. Well, I stopped her almost at once, although I found it extremely stimulating. I mean, this is the way homosexuals get their satisfaction, isn't it? In my view, it can't be right, can it? But what really frightens me is that for the few moments she was doing it, I really did enjoy it. Do you think I have homosexual tendencies? Please reply as soon as possible.

Probably few other aspects of sex are more misunderstood in our culture than oral lovemaking. There are very large numbers of couples who just do not know that men and women can use mouth-genital caresses during loveplay, while others, who are aware of it, reject it for a number of reasons, chief of which are that it is unhygienic, that it is unnatural, that it is unethical, or even, according to religious concepts, sinful.

First of all, for many centuries men and women in some cultures have been practising oral lovemaking, particularly in the Orient and in the warm southern countries of Europe. There is pictorial evidence still existing that the ancient Greeks and Romans practised it as a popular and stimulating loveplay, while Vatsayana describes the techniques in the *Kama Sutra,* the erotic Indian temple sculptures depict it, and there are erotic paintings, drawings and sculptures from Bali, Japan, China and Peru, to mention only a few, which illustrate both *cunnilingus* (the male's oral caresses of the female genitals) and *fellatio* (the female's oral caresses of the penis) both singly, and in positions (the most common of which is known as '69') in which each partner is stimulating the other simultaneously. In modern times, it has been an acceptable technique of stimulating among the French, the Italians and the Greeks. I was first introduced to it forty years ago by a fellow student at the Paris Sorbonne who, when I expressed surprise that she should do it, was as surprised at my surprise. 'But everyone does it!' she said, which was an exaggeration, but not all that great a one.

I think there are two reasons why we in the north have not practised it so freely, at least in modern times. Though the early and medieval Roman Catholic Church tried desperately to regulate the sexual behaviour of its flock, it went to such extremes that its requirements were outside the scope of healthy men and women to fulfil, and they simply did not try. After the Reformation, however, while the Protestants of the north were more far-sighted and not so extreme, they did introduce strictures on sexual behaviour, but these strictures could be attempted by most, e.g. the one position for coupling (man-above) and the denial of sexuality to women which removed the need for foreplay. This is one reason, and the other is our climate.

If I may digress for a brief moment. I believe our climate has been as much responsible for our being restricted in our lovemaking techniques as the guilt-feelings induced in us by our various religions. Loveplay that warrants the description cannot be performed under the heavy bedclothes that our icy bedrooms condemn us to use, nor can any other coupling position, except woman-above, rear-entry side-by-side – which is never as satisfactory as in the kneeling or standing postures – be successfully accomplished without both partners being outside the bedclothes, and getting half-frozen in the process, and certainly not enjoying the experience. I am quite certain that the huge improvement in the lovemaking techniques of increasing numbers of Englishmen is due to the increasing number of modern homes that have central heating.

Oral lovemaking cannot be carried out under bedclothes without the risk of one or both partners being smothered. And the remarks I have just made about general love-making techniques apply here also. So, not only has the climate restrained us from experimenting along these lines, but our puritan Protestantism, and particularly the sexual attitudes of our Victorian ancestors, has equally kept us from trying out the experiments, even if we thought of them.

Oral lovemaking then is not a new sexual technique which has come into being with the so-called permissive society. It is a technique almost as old as Man himself. In fact, it is probably older, because Kinsey, who was a zoologist before he turned his attention to humans, stated that most of the higher mammals incorporate it in their courtship procedures. It is, therefore, natural and bred into us, and we have suppressed it. On the other hand, Kinsey also noted in his report on male sexuality, that it was, at the time he made his survey, a more widespread activity than one credited. People just did not talk about it but when he asked they *admitted* it. What he actually wrote was: 'In marital relations, oral stimulation of the male or female genitalia occurs in about 60 per cent of the histories of persons who have been to college, although it is in only about 20 per cent of the histories of the high-school level and in 11 per cent of the histories of grade-school level . . . Because of the long-standing taboos in our culture on mouth-genital activity, it is quite probable that there has been more cover-up on this point than on most others in the present study.'

What is done by large numbers of people all over the world cannot, then, be unnatural or a deviation, especially as it has been done for many hundreds of years!

But is it sinful? That, I think, is a matter for personal conscience based on religious beliefs. Personally, I cannot see how it can possibly be either sinful or immoral. If a couple, no matter what their religious beliefs are, can square their consciences to use loveplay techniques which are designed to heighten sexual response, I can see no difference between fondling the penis or clitoris with the mouth and tongue and caressing a nipple with the fingers or mouth, or the clitoris with finger or penis; or, in coupling, between using the missionary position and a woman-above or rear-entry position.

Is it harmful to health, then? If the genitals are kept scrupulously clean – and genital hygiene is absolutely essential whether one uses oral lovemaking or not – they will have far, far fewer bacteria on and around them than there are in the mouth of a normal healthy person. What bacteria there are, are much less harmful to health than the bacteria carried by the mouth and anyone who rejects oral lovemaking on this ground must also reject ordinary mouth-to-mouth kisses, and certainly should avoid deep kissing at all costs.

What about the genital secretions? Neither the man's nor the woman's lubricating fluids has any taste or smell. That is an established medical fact. I have never known any man who practises cunnilingus complain on that score. Nor have any women written to me telling me that I am wrong about their partner's lubricating fluid.

When a woman has no religious, ethical or other scruples about performing fellatio but still cannot bring herself to do it, she may be able to accept the fact about the lubricating fluid, but still not be able to take her partner's penis into her mouth, because she finds the idea of receiving his semen in her mouth repugnant. Where this happens she either believes that it will harm her health if she swallows semen or that it will taste extremely unpleasant.

Semen swallowed cannot harm the health because it contains nothing that can possibly do so. Besides sperms, semen has as its ingredients fructose – simple sugar – which initiates and maintains the motility of the sperms, high concentrations of citric acid and ascorbic acid (vitamin C), a number of enzymes, bicarbonate and phosphate. Nor is it possible for woman to become pregnant if she swallows semen, which seems to be quite a widespread old wives' tale.

Women who do not fear the effects of swallowing semen often object that it will have an objectionable taste. While it is true that semen has a distinctive odour – which is imparted by the secretion of the prostate gland – I still maintain that when taken in the mouth it is not discernible. First of all, unless the woman feels with her lips the muscular spasms by which the semen is ejaculated or the partner gives other indications of having come off, it is very unlikely that she will know he has. The reasons for this are that she will be a very odd woman if sucking her partner's penis does not stimulate her, and practically all women (and men) when sexually roused produce excessive amounts of saliva. (It is this that tends to make deep kissing a rather messy business, however careful one tries to be.) The saliva is produced in such quantities that the addition of the half-teaspoonful – or even a teaspoonful if the man has not come off for five or six days previously and is particularly roused – is not noticeable.

I have been taken up on this point by a few women, but all I can say is that if they detect by the means I have just described, when the partner comes off, and believe they feel the semen spurting into the mouth, they are really imagining it. As I have mentioned from time to time, I have a group of collaborators who help me when I wish to carry out experiments or test a point such as this. The women of this group took special note over a period of two months of the occasions on which they believed they could detect semen in the mouth; 160 incidents were involved, out of which there were reports of 13 on which the woman said definitely she could detect it. Six of these incidents involved one woman; in other words, out of the 8 fellations to orgasm that she performed, only in two of them was she not aware of the arrival of the semen; and on closer investigation, she turned out to be one of those exceptions which prove the rule – her saliva production scarcely increases when she is sexually roused, and her salivary glands are not normally very active in any case.

At the same time that we carried out this experiment we also tested for another reaction on which I have been challenged by one or two women – that semen is not detectable by taste. Some women do complain that though the taste of semen is very mild indeed, it does slightly sting the back of the throat as it is swallowed. We found that this was true in roughly one-third of the incidents, and it was experienced by fourteen out of the twenty women who took part; but only in one case was it a permanent feature. We noted that in all cases, except this one, the men had urinated shortly before beginning to make love.

However, whether the semen is detectable or not as it is taken into the mouth or when it is swallowed, even those women who have complained to me that I am wrong in some of my assertions, all agreed that neither experience is unpleasant. That is the important point. Those who fear they may find it so will, I think, discover that once they have experienced it, they had no need to hesitate on those scores.

In any case, fellatio and cunnilingus are mostly used as a loveplay technique leading to eventual penis-vagina coupling. Both used to orgasm on occasions is a natural sequence of events, because, in my view, if the responses of either to these caresses of the partner become extremely intense, as they sometimes do, it would be foolish to spoil the climax by breaking the rhythm of the mounting sensations in order to couple. Anyhow, I think my views on substitutes for penis-vagina coupling permanently or preponderantly taking the place of penis-vagina coupling are known by this time – such response turns perfectly valid methods of stimulation techniques into deviations, mild ones, but nevertheless deviations.

I make two exceptions in this regard *vis-à-vis* fellatio and cunnilingus. First, there are a number of men suffering from partial impotence who respond to fellatio with full erection. However, as soon as they try to put the penis into the vagina they go limp. These men can almost invariably be brought off by the continuation of fellatio, and in this case I would say that it is perfectly valid if they are brought off in this way every time they make love. (As a matter of fact, I have recently heard from two men who have had full potency restored by a combination of the Masters and Johnson technique for partial impotence and fellation, i.e. instead of the manual stimulation of the penis by the partner as advised by Masters and Johnson, the partner has relied chiefly on fellatio to induce erection.)

Second, there are a number of women who suffer from delayed orgasm no matter how skilfully their partners stimulate them by other means, but who respond satisfactorily to cunnilingus. If, however, there is a pause in mouth stimulation while coupling is attempted, their sensations recede to zero, and refuse to come on again, whatever the partner does, yet if cunnilingus is resumed they can be brought to climax in a surprisingly short time. In such cases, too, I believe that it is valid for them to be brought off always in this fashion. I would suggest, however, that the lovemaking should conclude with penis-vagina coupling immediately *after* the woman has achieved orgasm, for the movements of the penis in the vagina will prolong her period of orgasmic afterglow, and she will have a sense of normality in lovemaking concluded in this way. By and large, since the man's response to stimulation is much more direct that the woman's, he is not so affected by the means by which he achieves climax, so long as the climax is fully satisfactory and satisfying. Psychologically, however, most women need to experience the penis in the vagina to be fully satisfied.

Finally, the man who objects to being fellated because it is what homosexuals do. So what? This reason seems to me wholly irrational and demonstrates an intolerance which is unworthy of a man who regards himself as normal. In any case, hundreds and thousands of heterosexual men, probably more than the number of homosexuals who do it, do it and enjoy it. I always suspect that men who protest in this fashion have an inkling that they may have homosexual tendencies which might come to the surface if they took part in this form of stimulation. In my view, it would be better if they stopped trying to repress such tendencies and tried to adjust to their situation. Certainly they would have happier sex-lives later on.

In fact, the male desire to be fellated is practically universal. There exists – and the woman should know this, recognise it and accept it – what is known as fellatio libido. That is to say that very many men have a strong sexual desire to be fellated. It is a perfectly normal male desire, and has nothing whatsoever to do with homosexual feelings or tendencies. Men who have a strong fellatio libido and whose partners refuse to co-operate with them, can and do become just as frustrated as men whose normal sexual desire is frustrated either by lack of opportunity to satisfy it by lovemaking or by incompetent stimulation by the partner, or her refusal to experiment sexually in any way. I find that the letters from men whose fellatio libido is strong and whose partners refuse their help are among the most distressing that I receive. It is all so pointless. Maybe the partner's objections are strongly based, but I do wish any woman who reads this, whose husband asks her to fellate him, will overcome her objections and co-operate. She will if she really loves him, and her reward will be immense. Believe me, I have recently seen two men whose fellatio libido is thwarted and who, as a consequence, have honestly and truthfully been almost reduced to nervous wrecks by it.

Let me repeat: Provided scrupulous cleansing of the

penis – especially if the man is not circumcised – is carried out, there is no taste or feel that can repel her. If she is really afraid of receiving semen in her mouth – and I can well understand that there may be some women in whom this is a very real fear – all she has to do is to tell her partner. He will understand and will readily agree to withdraw his penis if he feels he is on the verge of ejaculating. But, as I have said, couples who do use fellatio and cunnilingus as a regular feature of their lovemaking, in any case only occasionally stimulate each other in this way to orgasm.

I cannot speak for the woman's experience of cunnilingus, but I can speak from personal experience of fellatio, and I can say without hesitation, that with the exception of penis-vagina contact, it is the most intense and satisfying and the most voluptuous form of sexual stimulation there is – and I know no man or woman who disagrees with me, except one or two sadists and masochists, who find their own particular needs more rewarding. But it has to be done properly.

This means that the man has to know the anatomy and nerve-system of the clitoris, vaginal ridge and vaginal entrance intimately, and similarly the woman must know all there is to know about the nervous response of the penis.

When the woman is roused the outer and inner vaginal lips swell and the clitoris becomes erect and its head protrudes from its hood. No matter how small the clitoris is – and it varies in size from individual to individual as the penis does from man to man – if the vaginal lips are parted this small but extremely sensitive and powerful organ can be seen in a good light. (If it cannot be seen, then the woman ought to have a medical examination to discover if there are lesions preventing the head from protruding from the hood; if there are, a very simple operation, which both should insist is performed, can put matters right.) But the first thing for the man to do is to have a look at it. (I wonder how many men, even skilful lovers, have seen the clitoris? I have a suspicion, not many.) I advise this, because unless the man knows, through having seen it, exactly where the clitoris is, there are certain caresses which most women find highly stimulating which he will not be able to carry out effectively. Instead of being able to concentrate the tip of the tongue or the lips – even the teeth – on the clitoris head, he will merely fumble about in the general area.

Having visually located the clitoris-head, he should next locate with the tip of a finger or thumb, the shaft of the clitoris, which is about three-quarters of its entire length, and is buried in the flesh, but not so deeply that it cannot be felt. The shaft runs upwards into the apex of the outer lips and then bends slightly towards the pubic bone. It can be felt moving under the thin layer of flesh under slight pressure of the finger. The man should identify it by running his finger-tip up one side, round the end and down the other.

The clitoris-head, like the penis-head, is a concentrated mass of nerves, quite out of proportion with its size. They are not only connected with the woman's central sexual nervous system, so that any stimulation of them is felt throughout her complete sexual apparatus, but they come down into the vaginal ridge, where they spread out, take in the outer ring of the opening of the urethra, making that sensitive to light stimulation also, and go down to the vaginal entrance. This means that the whole vaginal ridge – and I call the *vaginal ridge* that part protected by the inner lips from clitoris to vagina-entrance – is sensitive, and that this sensitivity is imparted to the inner lips and the membrane lining of the outer lips.

Besides the tail-ends of the clitoral nerves sensitising the rim of the vagina-entrance, this has a nervous system of its own which is connected with the nerves of the perineum, that much neglected sensitive zone, which goes from the lower edge of the vaginal entrance to the anus in the woman, and from high up behind the scrotum to the anus in the man.

All this area from clitoris to anus is the man's field of

activity when he is performing cunnilingus. All of it responds to caresses with the tongue-tip and the lips to a much more intense degree than to caresses of the fingers or even the penis-head.

The penis-head is also highly responsive to caresses with the mouth and tongue. It, too, has a nervous system out of all proportion with its size, which is connected with his central sexual nervous system. It is particularly sensitive under and round the rim which the head forms with the shaft – the shaft, by the way, is scarcely sensitive at all – just below the urethral opening, and for most men, in the frenum, the little band of skin which connects the ordinary skin of the shaft to the membrane of the head, on the underside.

The scrotum is also responsive to licking and to *light* nips with the teeth. The perineum, which responds to heavy pressure of a finger at mid-point to such a degree that for most it will bring on erection, is also highly sensitive to light strokes of the tongue.

I am always surprised just a little by the woman's lack of imagination when it comes to stimulating her partner's penis and its surrounding area. (They make up for it once they have learned!) May I urge all women to be guided by their partner's directions? Don't forget, you women feel a much more general effect when you are stimulated, so that sensations spread over a large part of your body; while his sensations are concentrated in his penis and loins only, until he comes off. On the other hand, it is equally true that you may respond more to some caresses than to others, but that he may not know until you tell him.

In oral lovemaking we rely more than ever on my slogan for sex in general: Communicate, communicate, communicate!

If you will both communicate you will not be long in finding out how to caress penis and clitoris. The *Kama Sutra* gives some tips, and old Vatsayana knew what he was talking about. But perhaps I may add a few of my own just to provide a working basis.

Let's begin with fellatio. The woman should open her mouth widely, drawing her lips over her teeth as tightly as possible but not uncomfortably so. Fellation is neither kissing the penis, nor sucking it. It is oral friction, with the woman's head moving up and down and from side to side at the same time, rhythmically. It is important to bring the lips right back to the penis-tip at the end of the up-stroke, so that the lips and tongue can caress the rim; and it is equally important to drive down as deeply as possible on the down-strokes. Before going right down, the head can be sucked or pumped in and out of the mouth two or three times very slowly, but the important thing is to maintain the friction on the penis inside the lips.

There are one or two techniques of what I call fellatio-foreplay, which may be useful to know. These include holding the penis with the hand in such a position that the underside of the head is in close proximity to the tongue, which is run up and down from frenum-base to penis-opening lightly, either slowly or quickly; taking the frenum between the lips and rolling it between them as the man sometimes does when he is caressing a nipple; flicking at the tip just below the opening with very rapid darts of the tongue; if the opening is sizable, holding it open with the fingers and stroking the inside of it with the tip of the tongue; running the tip of the tongue right under the rim, from one side to the other; and making quick flicks all over the penis-head with the tongue-tip. Though the penis-shaft is not supposed to be very sensitive, some men find the tongue run up and down the underside from scrotum to tip and back again fairly slowly, but lightly, very stimulating.

Then there is the scrotum. The main thing to remember about it is that the testicles are extremely sensitive to pressure, and they and the scrotum itself must be treated gently. Light stroking of the scrotum's skin with the tongue is very pleasant, but it can be quite devastating if both testicles are drawn into and rolled round the mouth. *Very, very gentle* love-bites made on the skin of the scrotum can also be rousing.

I don't suppose there are many men who remain unresponsive to the following. The man lies on his back across the bed, with his buttocks as near to, or if possible a little over, the edge of the bed, his legs spread and drawn up towards his chest with the soles of his feet resting on the bed. This exposes the area of the perineum. The woman kneels on the floor, and beginning at the anus, she lightly runs her tongue-tip up the perineum, over the scrotum, up the underside of the penis, pauses at the frenum and penis-tip to flick at them, then retraces her steps, so to speak, down the penis, pauses for a second to nibble gently at the scrotum, then down the perineum to the anus. (All this is done several times in succession.) If she licks the anus lightly, so much the better. The anticipation of the caressing of penis-tip and anus at the end of each up and down stroke, can be almost devastatingly voluptuous.

The art of cunnilingus is just as skilled. Cunnilingus is licking and sucking, and is always usefully combined with strategically placed caresses of finger-tips. The woman helps her partner a great deal if she uses both her hands to draw back the vaginal lips as far as they will go, thus exposing the clitoris, vaginal ridge and entrance.

The clitoris itself is very responsive to quick light flicks with the tongue-tip, and some women find that if it is taken between the lips and sucked it will bring on a climax very quickly. Again there is cunnilingus foreplay. While he is flicking at the clitoris with tongue-tip, he should run a finger-tip up one side of the shaft, round and down the other, or take the shaft lightly between his fingers, draw back and release the clitoral hood rhythmically. After a few seconds of flicking at the clitoris, he should run his tongue down the vaginal ridge to the vaginal-entrance. There he should pause for a few seconds and run the tip of his tongue round the vaginal entrance, perhaps thrusting his tongue into the vagina as far as it will go, but I prefer this tonguing of the vagina as a separate technique. He should then go back up the vaginal ridge to the clitoris, whose shaft he has continued to stimulate with his finger or finger and thumb.

For some reason or other, which I cannot explain unless it is that the ridges on the tongue provide more friction than the smooth penis, many women respond ecstatically to the tongue being used as the penis. The man lies on his back and the woman kneels astride him with her genital area poised just above his mouth. Either she or he, preferably she, because that leaves his hands free to reach up to her nipples, draws the vaginal lips apart. He inserts his tongue into the vagina as far as it will go and then draws it back into his mouth, repeating this rhythmically and either slowly or quickly, as she wishes, every now and again running the tongue-tip round the entrance rim. She can if she wishes at the same time stimulate her clitoris with a finger.

If she takes up the same position that I described for the man, and he kneels on the floor, he can apply the same technique of stimulating the perineum, beginning with the anus and going up to the clitoris and back again.

It is best for the couple to experiment to discover the positions which suit them best when performing fellatio and cunnilingus. Both forms of stimulation can be carried out by one partner on the other, or by both partners simultaneously.

When deciding which position she should adopt the woman should always bear in mind that if her partner is younger than thirty-five or forty, his erect penis will stand up much closer to his belly than it will do after forty or forty-five, when it is likely to be horizontal to the ground, when he is himself standing upright. She must remember that if she has to depress it too far to get it into her mouth, she will hurt him. He will tell her if she does, and she must adjust her position accordingly. If the man goes down on his partner, about the most satisfactory position is if she lies on her back with her legs spread, her knees raised, a pillow, or perhaps two, under her buttocks, and he slides his body down towards the end of the bed, until his face is above her genital area.

She cannot, of course, fondle his penis manually in this position. If he wants her to do that, he should lie on his side beside her, his head towards her genital area and his penis within reach of one of her hands. But, as I say, the couple are best left to decide positions for themselves.

I would, however, like to describe one of the most satisfactory '69' positions for simultaneous fellatio and cunnilingus. The man lies on his back with his head about the middle of the bed. (He will have to draw up his knees if the bed has a foot-board.) She places herself above him, her head towards his penis, and her clitoral area over his face, taking her weight on her knees and elbows. With one hand he can part her vaginal lips, and use the other to stimulate her sensitive zones within reach, preferably a nipple.

Well, these are just a few hints. The combinations and variations are numerous. Each couple must experiment until they have found caresses and positions which suit them best. It could be, I imagine, a life's work to explore the whole technique thoroughly.

CHAPTER 8

Understanding the Sex-drive (Sex-urge)

THERE IS probably more misunderstanding about the sex-drive among men than about any other aspect of male sexual behaviour. It is understandable that men should be interested in the sex-drive, because it constitutes quite a large part of their male sex-image. I have referred several times to the man's assessment of his manhood, which means so much to him and which he judges by a number of factors, e.g. the strength of his erection, the size of his penis and his capacity, performance and success as a lover. To these must be added the sex-drive – that is, how often he wants to and can take part in sexual intercourse to orgasm. The more frequent is his desire, the more orgasms he can have in the shortest possible time, the more of a real man he is.

It is important that the man should have a proper understanding of the sex-drive for two reasons: first, he may expect too much, and develop feelings of inadequacy as a lover, which can in time affect his actual sexual functioning and his whole relationship with his partner; and second, that he should realise that frequency is not the criterion but that quality of performance is. So let us begin at the beginning and try to answer the question, *What is the sex-drive?*

The sex-drive is controlled by the interaction of various glands such as the pituitary and the testicles. The pituitary stimulates the testicles to produce the male sex hormone testosterone, and it is testosterone which, among other functions, actually sets up the physical tension which can only be relieved by sexual activity or orgasm, e.g. by masturbation or sexual intercourse. As you probably know, the man and the woman both produce male and female sex hormones. The man produces the male sex-hormones in greater quantity than the woman does, and the woman produces female sex-hormones in greater quantity than the man does. Nevertheless, though the woman produces less testosterone than the man, it is her testosterone production which controls her sex-drive.

Like everything else to do with sex, the sex-drive is not a constant. It not only varies from individual to individual, but in the same individual from occasion to occasion under the influence of a number of factors. Sexologists and others find it useful to set out guide-lines – and it must be stressed they are only guide-lines – for gauging the strength of the sex-drive. It will be useful, I think, if I set them down here, because it will help men who write to me, 'I am fairly highly-sexed, we make love twice a week,' or 'The trouble is I'm only averaged-sexed, and can't really make love more than once a day,' to find their own level, so to speak.

On the whole, the great majority of men and women, if they leave it to nature, are sexually roused and must find an outlet for their tension in one way or another, between three and five times a week. Those active to this degree are designated AVERAGE-SEXED. On either side of this majority, there are two groups, ones whose sex-drive prompts them to have more or fewer outlets than average. Some men and women, for example, not only need a daily outlet, but a twice or thrice daily outlet; and anyone who has the need for six or more outlets a week is termed HIGHLY-SEXED. On the other hand, there are men and women who only need one outlet a week, or one a fortnight, or one a month. Those who make love under the influence of their sex-drive once a week or less frequently, are termed LOW-SEXED.

There are differences in experience of response to stimulation and in the intensity of the orgasm-sensations between the three main classifications. The highly-sexed are much less inhibited than the other two types. For them sex is a very prominent part of their overall living; for them penis and vagina are as valid working-parts of their bodies as are their hands and legs; and somehow this acceptance of sex, inevitable though it is, swamps feelings of guilt and shame – if any ever raised their ugly heads, which few can complain of – while feelings of inadequacy certainly are unknown among them.

They run into trouble only if they are unwise enough, and some of them are, to select partners who are quite unable to meet their sexual needs, or have inhibitions which prevent them from co-operating in sexual activity with the same happy, nonchalant and utterly complete out-giving.

Because of this free approach to lovemaking, the highly-sexed respond more easily to stimulation and have highly intense orgasms. For many of them, the orgasm-sensations are so intense that as they are coming off, they involuntarily moan, whimper, cry out loudly, scratch or bite, shudder violently from head to foot, arch their backs, double their pulse-rates and breathe as though they were the victims of very acute bronchitis, and at the peak of the orgasm some lose consciousness for a second or two. Naturally, they experiment much more freely and indulge in far more extreme forms of sexual behaviour. They never become bored with sex, therefore, and though their frequency may fall off a little, they continue their lovemaking into their late seventies and eighties.

The low-sexed, in contrast, are susceptible to responses which in the highly-sexed would be barely noticeable. Because their natural desire urges them to make love infrequently, they seem to have less encouragement to experiment, probably as a result of which they give the impression of having little or no interest in sex altogether.

The average-sexed, who constitute the vast majority of

men and women, have a harder time than either of their low- or highly-sexed fellows. To make their sex-lives really satisfying and satisfactory, they need a higher degree of performance than the low-sexed and it does not come to them so easily as it does to the highly-sexed. They have to be encouraged, in one way or another, from one source or another, to experiment, and to do so to any worthwhile extent they often have to overcome obstacles in the form of their own or their partner's inhibitions. Nevertheless, they are capable of achieving far more stable relationships than the highly-sexed, once they have worked out their own sexual pattern.

There is a tendency on the part of the average-sexed to look askance at the high sexual activity of the highly-sexed, regarding them as sex-mad. (To the low-sexed the highly-sexed are a rather bewildering enigma.) They also tend to despise the low-sexed, whom they regard as poor specimens of human beings. Their attitude to the highly-sexed is motivated by envy; they will realise this once they are honest enough to admit it; and their attitude to the low-sexed is motivated by pride in their own superior activity and sexual achievement.

It is essential to remember, therefore, that the object of all responses to the sex-drive is to obtain relief as complete as possible from the tensions which the sex-drive creates. In other words, to obtain the fullest satisfaction through lovemaking and orgasm which the strength of one's own sex-drive makes possible. It does not matter how often or how infrequently a couple make love; what does matter enormously is that they are sexually satisfied by their love-making. The low-sexed is just as satisfied by his one orgasm every ten days or so, as the highly-sexed is by his two or three orgasms a day.

By and large, the sex-drive is at its peak between twenty-one and forty in men, and twenty-five and forty-five in women. Some authorities state that the peak is reached in the male between fifteen and eighteen. I am inclined to dispute this. I believe that these authorities are confusing sexual activity with sexual need as determined by the sex-drive. While it is true that many boys are more sexually active as adolescents than they are as adults, more often than not adolescent boys deliberately seek sexual experience through masturbation, heavy petting or intercourse simply because sex is a new experience for them and they are anxious to learn as much about it as quickly as they can. Many factors pleasantly conspire to keep sex constantly in the fore-front of the boy's adolescent experience. His capacity for erection is instantaneous; three or four rubs of the frenum and penis-head will bring about full erection in fifteen to twenty seconds, and if he lacks experience of activity with the opposite sex, his fertile imagination conjures up highly erotic fantasies which have no relation with actuality, but which produce strong (cerebrally induced) erections at the swish of a skirt or a glimpse of half a breast. Unless he is naked his erection draws his attention to his penis by the pressure exerted on it by underpants and trousers; very often if he is naked, his attention will be immediately drawn to his penis because the images in his brain cause such an engorgement of the penis by blood, that the penis aches. Once his attention is drawn to the penis, the desire to touch it is almost irresistible and it is only a matter of moments before he experiences the exquisite novel climax of his attentions. Few adult men, especially after the age of thirty, except in the case of the very highly sexed, can have similar experiences.

The adolescent, therefore, does not respond solely to his sex-drive. The same is true of most adults. It is surely the experience of all of us that we go to bed with no sexual tension present at all, i.e. we are not under the influence of our sex-drive, and we have no thought whatsoever of making love. Then all of a sudden we find we are making love, our desire to do so having been triggered off by something we have done or said, or something our partner has said or done – the brushing of a thigh or buttock against the penis, an unintentional touch of a hand on a breast, a kiss of some indefinable subtle content or even a half-whispered 'I love you!' This happens at all times of life. In fact, in later life it is no excuse for a man to shelter behind a weakened sex-drive to avoid sex; a man is capable at all times of being directly stimulated, by the partner's hand or his own, to full erection, and the quality of the lovemaking, physically and emotionally, is none the worse for it.

After middle age, the sex-drive does slow down a little, and the urge to make love becomes less frequent. On the other hand, it is quite wrong to think that it will disappear altogether. There is no reason at all why the average-sexed and the highly-sexed man (and woman) should not make love right through old age. The highly-sexed almost certainly will without having given it a conscious thought; the average-sexed really need not to allow themselves to become sexually lazy. The sex-drive of the low-sexed, it would seem, fades out earlier and more completely. Masters and Johnson, the American sex-investigators, have recently discovered that the earlier a man or woman become sexually active – beginning with masturbation – and the more active they are in their peak years – not always responding to their sex-drive – they will remain active much longer in later life.

I am often asked why, if testosterone controls the sex-drive, and since synthetic testosterone is available, it is not possible to increase the strength of the sex-drive (in other words, its frequency of operation) by injections or implants of this hormone. This cannot be done before the age of fifty-five in the man, and until after the menopause in the woman. The trouble is that if testosterone is injected or implanted in a man whose testicles are producing testosterone at their own level, the extra testosterone reacts in such a way that the pituitary stops the testicles from working, consequently, after a time the testicles shrink and atrophy, and will not produce testosterone again. Not only that, but other problems which I need not mention here, also arise.

Injections or implants of testosterone can, however, be effective in cases of late-middle-aged men whose testicles have stopped producing testosterone and have shrunk in size. The sex-drive can be restarted and there can be quite a dramatic change in the size of the testicles. Unfortunately not every man responds to injections and implants at all, so one cannot say that they are a 'cure' for loss of sex-drive. Medical opinion also differs about their efficacy or even the wisdom of prescribing them. American doctors are enthusiastic about their use, British doctors on the whole are not. They are not available on the N.H.S., but a number of doctors will prescribe them privately. The cost, however, is very high.

The main thing to remember is that one is not dependent on one's sex-drive for one's sexual activity or for one's enjoyment of sex. The psychological approach to sex is a very powerful factor in maintaining sexual performance, and if the right mental approach to lovemaking is always the chief consideration, the sex-drive can be left to take care of itself.

CHAPTER 9

What Is Normal Sex?

Dear Mr Chartham, My husband keeps asking me to let him have intercourse with him going into me from behind. I have refused so far, because I don't think it can be right. What I mean is, men and women have been so made that they can make love facing one another, so why should anyone want to copy the only way animals can do it? But Ken keeps insisting I've got hold of the wrong end of the stick. He says that there must be variety in a couple's sex-life, otherwise they get bored and fall out of love. He says there can be nothing wrong in couples making love from behind, because if they weren't intended to do it, they wouldn't be made so that they could do it. I love Ken very much, and I would like to do as he suggests, but just can't because I don't think it's normal. However, he has persuaded me to write and ask you what your views are. If you say it's all right, I have half-promised to do what he wants.

Dear Dr Chartham, I would dearly like to perform cunnilingus on my wife and have her perform fellatio on me, but she absolutely refuses. She says it's filthy and disgusting, and practically called me a pervert for just suggesting it. But these are quite normal practices between husband and wife, aren't they?

Dear Dr Chartham, I am 21 and my husband is

23, and we have been married for five months. We had sex before we got married. Only occasionally we had full intercourse with Johnny using a french letter, because I couldn't get fixed up with the Pill and somehow never got round to getting a diaphragm cap fitted, so we used to rely on heavy petting. But now I am on the Pill. In spite of this, there are still times when Johnny asks me to bring him off by hand, and wants to bring me off in the same way. I think this is kinky. I mean there's such a difference between the experience of masturbating and full intercourse. I can't see why anyone who isn't kinky should prefer masturbation when he can have intercourse. What do you think?

Dear Mr Chartham, I am rather worried because my husband seems always to be wanting to make love. We have been married for sixteen months. I am 25 and my husband is 27. We did not actually make love before we married, but during our courting days I had an idea that my boy-friend, as he was then, was quite passionate by nature, by the way he kissed me and caressed me. I didn't mind it. To be quite honest, it was one of the exciting things I found about him.

In the few months after we married, we made love almost every day. This didn't worry me either, because in the excitement of being married to the man I loved, I was quite ready and willing to be made love to whenever he wanted to. I knew, though, this wasn't the real sexual me, because from the time I first became aware of having any sexual desire, I don't suppose I felt the need to masturbate more than half-a-dozen times a year, and being roused sexually six or seven times a week was, I was sure, my way of reacting to this new, wonderful experience of being married. Mind you, I had expected to have an increase in desire, but not to this extent.

In the same way, I thought my husband was reacting to this new experience in the same way, and that, in time, he would, so to say, get the novelty out of his system and settle down sexually. This hasn't happened. Well, I suppose it has to a small extent, because we make love on average five times a week, while in the early days it was often seven or more, and never less than six.

Don't you think making love so often is not good for a man who has quite a heavy and responsible job? How often ought one to make love? I don't mean a set round figure per week, but the rough normal average.

Dear Robert, I am very worried about my wife. We haven't been married very long and before we were married Alice wouldn't say boo to a goose, so you will understand why I am worried when she keeps asking me to walk about our bedroom naked when I've got an erection. I don't mind her seeing me naked when I haven't got an erection, but having an erection and letting her see it is a bit embarrassing. I've told her I don't mind walking about when I haven't got an erection, but she says that's no good. She says the size of my penis when it's erect and the way it nods backwards and forwards as I move makes her very excited. This I know is true, because when I do eventually join her in bed it's unmistakable that she's roused. Surely it isn't normal for a woman to want to be excited in such a way. I suppose I would lose my embarrassment in time, and I'm prepared to do any-thing to please her, so long as I know I'm not encouraging any bad habit. What do you think about it?

These letters reveal what a confusion there is in men's and women's minds about what is 'normal' sex-behaviour and what they think may be perverted, or as I prefer to call it, deviant. Actually I have letters which refer to practically every form of sexual activity with the exception of intercourse in the man-above-face-to-face position – making love in the bath, making love in front of a mirror, making love standing up, rubbing the penis in the armpits or between the breasts, fingering the anal sphincter, even the woman initiating lovemaking and taking the active role right through to orgasm.

What people do not seem to realise is that it is the responsibility of each partner to provide for the other in lovemaking the most pleasurable and exciting sensations of physical stimulation and arousal so that when orgasm eventually arrives it is accompanied by the most intense sensations that mood, circumstances and the love-skills of the partner will allow. If a couple are using their lovemaking to express in tangible, physical terms the reason for love-making – then every session should be conducted along these lines. Not only that – every kind of caress, every aid, every act which will enhance the partner's experience must be permissible and cannot be wrong. Since the variety of aids to this end is so great, and men's and women's responses are so individual, it is nonsense to talk about 'normal' sex.

To put it more emphatically: *There is no sexual caress that a man can apply to his wife or a wife to her husband, that cannot be considered 'normal', provided both partners find them pleasant and sexually stimulating.*

What I have written about caresses applies equally to positions for coupling. With the possible exception of anal intercourse, in which the penis is inserted in the anus, and which is illegal in Great Britain, even between husband and wife, there is no position for coupling which is not normal.

The rule I have just set out for caresses can be extended to a general rule:

There is nothing a man and woman can do with one another in lovemaking from the first caress to final coupling that is not normal, provided neither partner is compelled to do anything against his/her will.

In other words, it is difficult, if not impossible, for husband and wife, fiancé and fiancée, man and woman to do anything that is not *sexually* normal. This being so, since the overriding desire of both is to please the other partner, those who find they have doubts should allow themselves to be coaxed and persuaded to put them aside.

'But half a minute!' I can hear someone protesting. 'You've just said, "There is *nothing* a man and woman can do with one another in lovemaking that is not normal". You must be joking. What about real perversions like fetishism or sadism or masochism or transvestism?'

My rule still applies — *always provided that neither partner is compelled to do something against his/her will.* Take fetishism, for example. What harm can be done if a man wants to make love with his boots on or in a rubber mackintosh, or have his partner wear nothing but a feather boa and a string of pearls *so long as the partner takes part in lovemaking in these conditions of her own free will?* The boots, the mackintosh, the feather boa and the pearls can do her no physical harm, and by wearing them herself or letting her partner wear them, she will have allowed him to obtain the object of all good lovemaking — sexual satisfaction and gratification, and is not only expressing her love for him, but allowing him to express his love for her. If he can only do this by using objects or fantasies and *she does not mind his using them,* how can anyone argue that he should be denied such aids merely because not everyone has to use them.

The same is true of sadism and masochism. Despite their often frightening appearance, the chains and the thongs and the cats-o'-nine-tails are more symbolic to the sadist and masochist than instruments of torture. Only very very rarely indeed does the sadist inflict serious harm (or any harm at all) on his partner and *if his partner takes part in his amateur dramatics entirely of her own free will* — and she will rarely consent to do so unless she has the complementary opposite desires, i.e. is a masochist – who is to deny either the effects of their strange wishes, the expression of their love through their lovemaking?

What harm can a man do his wife by dressing up in women's clothes, provided he does so in the privacy of their home, and does nothing which will bring him into conflict with the law, e.g. go into the streets? Transvestism is widely misunderstood. More transvestites are completely heterosexual than are homosexual. If the partner can be assured that her husband is not using his longings except to achieve satisfaction for his sexual urges in heterosexual intercourse, she can make her own sexual experience so much richer by accepting his fancies and helping him to work out his fantasies. But she must not be compelled to accept them; she must be sincerely assured that so long as she does not mind her husband's oddness neither is doing wrong.

Someone once asked me, 'But surely you can't mean that you apply your rule to such disgusting deviations as urolagnia, coprophilia and osphresiophilia?'

But why not? So long as the partner co-operates of his/her own free will, and these practices are carried out in strict privacy so that no one else is offended, it would do more harm to deny them and it can do immeasurable good to permit them.

Many women write to me worried by occasional heavy petting to orgasm within marriage. I am all in favour of it if it is practised only occasionally. There are occasions when during foreplay the rhythm of the mounting sensations is so exquisitely voluptuous that it would be madness to break into them in order to couple. In these circumstances reaching orgasm by mutual simultaneous masturbation is as valid a way of terminating intercourse as is penis-vagina contact.

In my view, it is only when a couple become so fixated on mutual masturbation that they *never* terminate intercourse with penis-vagina contact that I regard their behaviour as deviant. But here again I have to make an exception. There are a number of men and women who can only be brought off by masturbation. Who is to deny them release of their sexual tensions by prohibiting them from always terminating their lovemaking in this way? Certainly not me.

Finally, a word about anal intercourse; and here I have to confess to a personal hang-up. I cannot for the life of me understand why a couple should make use of a canal whose proper function is not to receive the penis and which does not provide the qualities of sensation that the vagina does, when the vagina is so near. I do not understand it; it is not for me. And yet I know there are couples who get great satisfaction from it—so I cannot condemn them, either.

CHAPTER 10

'How Can I Tell Her?'

Dear Mr Chartham [a young woman in her middle twenties, married seven years, wrote to me this morning] . . . what worries me is that my need and desire for sex have increased, while my husband's has not. I have always enjoyed it, but it is only in the last three years that I have felt such a need for intercourse. Unfortunately, once or maybe twice a week is all my husband needs and wants, and this makes me at times almost invariably frustrated and consequently bad-tempered. *We don't talk about sex* [my italics]. On the one occasion when I tried to explain how I felt, he became upset and decided he was inadequate and that I would soon be having an affair. Since then I have been afraid to say anything because I don't want to upset him.

There was more in this letter which I cannot disclose without breaking my firm rule that nobody else sees the letters that are written to me in confidence, but I can say that a serious situation is building up that can ultimately threaten the whole marriage, and what is so unfortunate is that it could be avoided if only the couple could discuss their sexual lives frankly with one another.

After seven years of marriage this couple are still not talking to one another about sex! I wish I could say that this kind of letter is rare among the dozens of letters I receive every week, but unhappily they arrive only too often.

Sometimes it is men who complain that they cannot discuss sex with their wives; sometimes it is wives complaining of their husband's reticence. But whichever partner is at fault, in this lack of communication lies one of the more common grounds for much sexual and marital unhappiness.

Part of the reason for this lack of communication is undoubtedly the awkward artificial vocabulary which sexual matters have, from the Latin names of some of the organs, through to the word orgasm. (Does there exist, I wonder, a man or a woman who inquires of the partner, 'Are you approaching orgasm?' rather than saying, 'Are you coming?'?) Many men and women do not even know these quasi-medical and pseudo-medical terms, but are aware that the four-letter words for them are not used between 'nice' people. It is for this reason that I have tried to use as few of the recognised technical terms and phrases as possible in my books and other writings, and substituted words and phrases of my own or those sometimes used by others. I would much prefer to use the four-letter words, but to do so would be an affront to many, even if I were not charged by the authorities with obscenity. One can only hope that the four-letter words will be returned to their former currency in decent vernacular speech and writing, but that seems to me some way off even in our so-called 'permissive society', and however much we may strive towards what Mr. Roy Jenkins has called 'a civilised society'.

Another part of the reason for the lack of communication between couples about sex is the background and environment in which they have been generally reared. This inhibits many men and women from expressing themselves fully in their sexual activities. It is almost as if while making love, they are attempting to convince themselves that sex does not exist, or if it does it is merely the result of an irresistible biological urge.

They are partly right, of course, because physical sex is irresistible to the average man and woman – only those who dedicate their lives to celibacy seem able to gain any degree of control over their sexual urges which enables them to desist from any physical self-expression of their biological reactions – but by denying any contact of love with sex they are denying their alleged superiority over the animal world. This sexual superiority is inherent in Man by his ability to excite himself sexually at will and in Woman by her capability of becoming sexually roused at any time and not merely when she is ovulating, that is, producing a mature egg. Those who make love purely to relieve the physical tensions which the chemistry of their sexual apparatus builds up, are, in fact, denying their manhood and womanhood.

Throughout all my writings on physical sex I have stressed over and over again that lovemaking should be exactly what it says it is – making love. By using physical sex as the supreme expression of the emotional love the partners profess to have for one another, they elevate the physical activity to the higher plane of the emotions. Neither partner has any hesitation in saying to the other, 'I love you', 'I adore you', 'I worship the ground you walk on', when expressing the emotional love he or she feels, and I cannot for the life of me understand why they should not be able to say to one another, 'I love making love with you'. But if you could see the number and variety of complaints I receive because their partners have never expressed any enjoyment of intercourse in any of its phases, and feel unable to break the ice in this connection themselves because they feel that the partner would be embarrassed if they did; if, as I say, you could see the number of complaints I alone receive, you would appreciate how very few couples there are who are able to make even this simple, but extremely comforting confession.

Most couples are sensible enough in these days to discuss before marriage how they intend to plan their family. There is considerable evidence that this is a widespread practice, but it appears that they do so only in terms of contraception, generally about whether the woman shall go on The Pill, or use a device such as the diaphragm cap or intra-uterine device, or loop. If only they could carry this discussion just one step further and talk about love-making even a little it would be a beginning, and once they had started they would, I am sure, find that they would be able to develop their language of sex as their technique of lovemaking developed.

It is surprising how many of us, even among the young, are still inhibited by the deeply ingrained attitudes of our Victorian forbears to sex. One young man of twenty-five who, I know from personal experience, can discuss sexual matters with men-friends in a vocabulary which reveals a mastery of four-letter words and a frankness that denies all inhibitions in that context, recently approached me for advice over a small problem. He was not inexperi-enced sexually before he married two years ago, but since marriage he has, I know, settled down sexually and to all appearances – and I am sure in reality – very happily so.

'Robert,' he said, 'both of us enjoy our lovemaking enormously, but recently when we have been having a very successful session, I've wanted Jane to hold my testicles while I come off.'

'Then why don't you tell her so?' I suggested.

'How can I?' he exclaimed. 'I'd feel a fool saying to her, "Hold my testicles, dear". It's such a funny word, testicles, and I can't possibly say to her, "Hold my balls". I just couldn't use that word to her.'

'Why not?' I said. 'I've heard you use it often enough.'

'But that's not the same. It's a man's word. A man understands what you're saying.'

'If you think Jane wouldn't understand maybe you have a surprise in store if you ever do use it.'

'But it's not a word one uses in front of a woman, and certainly not to one's wife!'

'How strong is this feeling you have?' I asked.

'Very strong,' he admitted. 'In fact, I'm beginning to

feel quite frustrated about it, and that's what's really worrying me – that I'll develop a complex about it.'

From the tone of his voice and the expression on his face, I could see that it was a serious matter for him.

'Look here,' I said, 'I'd far rather you told her what you want, but if you really can't, then what's wrong with taking her hand and putting it there?'

'Yes,' he replied. 'That might do the trick. Thanks.'

In contrast with this young man, I know several couples who can talk quite freely to one another about sex, and who use four-letter words in doing so. None knows that I know others who have developed the same practice, yet all have said in words something like this, 'It's strange how the four-letter words you would never dream of using in mixed company become quite normal and natural after a time.'

Tied up with this problem of non-communication, I am quite certain, is the still prevalent habit of the majority of Anglo-Saxon couples at all events, of making love mostly at night, or in the morning, in complete darkness, or with the curtains drawn and in semi-darkness, if they make love in the afternoons. (Or making love only in bed, and never anywhere else but the bedroom.) Those who cannot make love in the light are not only missing a great deal, for sight is a great stimulant, especially for the man, though less so for the woman – many women keep their eyes closed throughout lovemaking, but few men do – but are pandering to the concept that physical sex is if not disgusting, then not quite nice, and fit only to be performed in circumstances which prevent the performance from being seen. If couples made love in a light good enough to enable them to see one another, I am quite sure they would have less inhibition about talking of it more easily.

My young friend who wanted his wife to hold his testicles after he had put his penis into her vagina and while he came off, was not alone, by a very long chalk, in having special techniques which he wishes his wife would adopt, and the denial of which builds up into physical sensations that, like his sexual tension itself, if not relieved causes feelings of frustration. These feelings of frustration, if not overcome in some way, even become so acute that lovemaking eventually turns sour and with it the marriage.

As I have said elsewhere, both men and women have some quite mistaken views of one another's personalities and particularly in the sphere of sex. Some of the bawdiest-minded men I know, restrain their bawdy talk in the company of their wives, because they regard 'the little woman' as a frail flower, to be cossetted and protected from all nastiness. What they do not seem to realise is that very few women are as frail as all that. Left in circumstances which withdraw the husband's protection, there are not many women who are not able to look after themselves quite adequately.

I am certainly not advocating that men should not curb their bawdiness in front of their wives; what I am trying to get over is that there are very few women, no matter how sheltered their pre-marriage background was, who cannot be taught by degrees, to be frank and forthcoming not only in their sexual techniques, but in talking about sex. Similarly, I am quite certain that there really are few men who, if gradually broken in, would be embarrassed by such frankness in their wives, but who, on the contrary, would welcome it.

By and large, men are more adventurous and courageous sex-wise than are women. Modesty is a desirable quality in a woman, but it has no place in practical sex. But as the men are bolder and less inhibited than most women, and are still – in spite of all I have written over the past five years! – regarded generally as the aggressors in sex, it is usually up to them to make the first moves in establishing communication. While they do so, however, they must do nothing which *might* offend the susceptibilities of their partner. Above all they should move slowly, feeling their way, as it were, noting their wives' reactions to certain words or phrases, just as they gradually initiate more and more sophisticated techniques of foreplay.

A good way of establishing the principle of communicating about sex is for the man to say what is in his mind as he makes love to his partner. In other words, he says his thoughts aloud. He may begin the lovemaking by saying so in so many words—'I want to love you' or some such phrase as may come more naturally to him. Then as he caresses throat or thighs or belly he will describe the various parts of the body as they appear to him as felt through the 'rosy hue of sexual tension'. Before he begins to caress her nipple with his mouth, let him say what he is going to do; when he is caressing her clitoris with a finger, let him say, for example, how soft and warm and secret it is. All the time he gives the impression that he is speaking to himself.

Alternatively, he may tell his partner how thrilling her caresses of him are. Simple phrases, such as 'That's good! Oh, that's good!' whispered or murmured with sincerely genuine appreciation are all that is needed.

Admittedly there is a difficulty about referring to certain organs by name. Personally, I can accept penis naturally, but I have to reject *testicles*, *scrotum*, *clitoris* and *vagina* as being too artificial. If others have the same difficulty and find themselves inhibited from using the four-letter words, then let them give such parts terms of their own choice. One couple I know refer to the penis as John, the clitoris as Little John and the vagina as Mary. I know this looks whimsical in cold print on the cold page, just as what I have suggested in the preceding paragraphs may seem to some too ridiculous to contemplate. But in the warmth of affection, the privacy of lovemaking and the desire to demonstrate one's emotional love by one's physical acts, they sound quite differently.

If the wife, after a time, makes no vocal response, he can draw her into doing so by asking her if the caress he is making is pleasing her. 'Is that good?', 'Do you like that?' Even if her only reply is a whispered 'yes', it is a beginning.

If she merely nods her head, he should repeat his question or put it in another way, until she does whisper her assent.

After a month or two, he can ask her if there is anything he does to her during foreplay she likes particularly, or finds the contrary of stimulating, or if there is anything he is omitting to do which she would like him to do to her. From the beginning he should somehow make it necessary for her to tell him when she is ready to receive the penis, gently refusing to react to a signal as far too many couples do, or accept the responsibility of judging when they shall couple.

Gradually the husband will find that the silence-barrier is being broken in greater and greater depth, until both are able to react vocally to lovemaking, and from that graduate to being able to discuss their sexual activities and everything to do with their sex-lives even when they are NOT making love. The approach to this final stage can be initiated if need be, by the husband going up behind his wife when she is engaged in some not very important chore, putting his hands over her breasts, and telling her what beautiful breasts she has, kissing the nape of her neck as he does so; or running his hands over her thighs while making similar complimentary remarks.

All that I have said up to now in relation to the husband can apply to the wife who feels the need for communicating with a silent husband. She can do this in two ways: either by exclaiming how thrilling his caresses are, or by admiring his body, and especially his penis and the strength of his erection. She should adopt the same techniques as I have advised him to use to make him speak, rather than reply by gestures. Personally, I do not think any lovemaking is complete without both telling the other how good it was, as they cuddle up together in the afterglow of orgasm.

As I have explained, the object of communicating sex-wise is to make for absolute frankness between the couple in their sexual lives, so that all otherwise secret inhibitions are dispersed and a cause of sexual irritation removed. The couple who have this ability to communicate have no difficulty in experimenting with and enlarging their range of lovemaking techniques, thereby expanding their lovemaking continually and leaving no place for boredom to creep in and eventually destroying their sexual lives and perhaps ruining their marriages.

One final reminder – make it a firm rule to make love with the light on more often than you make love in the dark. Light and talking go together.